THE CENTER DID NOT HOLD

D0615019

THE CENTER DID NOT HOLD

A BIDEN/OBAMA BALANCE SHEET

Robert Eisenberg

OR Books

New York · London

© 2021 Robert Eisenberg

Published by OR Books, New York and London
Visit our website at www.orbooks.com

All rights information: rights@orbooks.com

All rights reserved. No part of this book may be reproduced or transmitted in any form or by any means, electronic or mechanical, including photocopy, recording, or any information storage retrieval system, without permission in writing from the publisher, except brief passages for review purposes.

First printing 2021

Cataloging-in-Publication data is available from the Library of Congress.
A catalog record for this book is available from the British Library.

Typeset by Lapiz Digital Services. Printed by BookMobile, USA, and CPI, UK.

paperback ISBN 978-1-68219-307-5 • ebook ISBN 978-1-68219-253-5

To Bella, Erwin, and Baki

CONTENTS

ACKNOWLEDGMENTS

I would like to acknowledge the great assistance in the writing of this book given to me first and foremost by Cindy Connolly, and by Eli Mishulovin.

INTRODUCTION

President Barack Obama and Vice President Joe Biden left a lingering bad taste in the mouths of many progressives who had high hopes for their administration. With the advantage of hindsight since his departure from the White House, Obama can be characterized as a cautious centrist, not a bold progressive. As for Vice President Joe Biden, his fifty-year career in politics is marked by a hawkish stance on both foreign policy and crime. This book revisits over one hundred issues dealt with—or obstinately not dealt with—by the Obama–Biden administration and comes to the following conclusions:

- On many issues Obama and Biden did not take a progressive position but instead passively allowed the opportunity to initiate change to slip by.
- On other issues they took a conservative position.
- On still other issues on which they took a progressive stance, many were, in the end, rejected by a conservative Congress, or overturned by the courts. President Donald Trump also rescinded many of Obama's executive orders.

The number of progressive changes under the Obama–Biden administration were meager indeed. Either the impetus for change somehow fizzled or was retroactively blocked and, in the end, scant progress was made.

There was some good news. Homicides and violent crimes trended downward during the Obama–Biden years. Inflation was tame, infant mortality rates declined in states that accepted Medicaid expansion, and the jobless rate dropped below its historical median. The number of federal prisoners declined. First Lady Michelle Obama led the charge to set new nutrition standards for schools. Her "Let's Move!" initiative promoted exercise, and she advocated for the Healthy, Hunger-Free Kids Act, which passed in 2010. Finally, there was the successful bail-out of the auto industry, potentially saving many thousands of jobs, albeit at the expense of initiating a two-tiered wage system.

But beyond the few issues that trended positive under Obama and Biden, and the rare progressive successes that "stuck," they have little to point to with pride. The entries in this book represent a disap-pointing legacy. With Joe Biden having defeated Trump in the 2020 presidential election, the time is ripe for a close assessment of the administration in which he served as vice president.

PART I

DEMOCRACY

Transparency

On his very first day in office, President Barack Obama expressed a commitment to "creating an unprecedented level of openness in government," and announced a series of transparency-related reforms.[1] These measures included expediting the process of obtaining records under the Freedom of Information Act (FOIA). Obama sent a memo to federal agencies with assurances that the administration would work with them "to ensure the public trust and establish a system of transparency, public participation, and collaboration."[2] But by March 2010, a mere year later, the Associated Press found that seventeen major agencies under Obama were 50 percent more likely to reject FOIA requests than under his immediate predecessor.[3] Records that were released were typically redacted, sometimes heavily, with a black felt-tipped pen obscuring contents deemed to be secret.

An AP analysis of 2014 federal data found that the Obama administration refused a record number of times to turn over files that might be especially newsworthy, said more regularly than any prior administration that it couldn't find documents, and took longer than ever to turn over any files when it provided them.[4] An unprecedented 714,231 requests for information were recorded that year. According to the AP, the administration spent an unprecedented $434 million in response to the requests, and $28 million on lawyers' fees to keep records secret.

The AP determined in 2017 that during its final year, the Obama administration spent even more, $36.2 million, "on legal costs defending its refusal to turn over federal records under the Freedom of

---

1   https://obamawhitehouse.archives.gov/the-press-office/transparency-and-open-government

2   https://obamawhitehouse.archives.gov/the-press-office/transparency-and-open-government

3   https://www.latimes.com/archives/la-xpm-2010-mar-21-la-na-ticket21-2010mar21-story.html

4   https://www.pbs.org/newshour/nation/obama-administration-sets-new-record-withholding-foia-requests

Information Act," and broke another record for "times federal employees responded to requests by saying they couldn't find a single page of information."[5]

Meanwhile, the *Columbia Journalism Review*, among others, noted that the Obama years had witnessed the prosecution of more leakers than had all of the previous presidential administrations combined.[6] As for bona fide whistleblowers under the Obama watch, twice the number were prosecuted under provisions of the 1917 Espionage Act than under all previous presidents combined.

5   https://www.ap.org/ap-in-the-news/2017/obamas-final-year-us-spent-36-million-in-records-lawsuits

6   https://www.cjr.org/criticism/barack_obamas_press_freedom_legacy.php

Binney, Drake, Loomis, Wiebe

President Obama employed the Woodrow Wilson-era Espionage Act a record eight times during his first term. He used it against officials suspected of leaking classified information.

Four intelligence figures who felt morally compelled to become whistleblowers were William Binney, Thomas Drake, Edward Loomis, and J. Kirk Wiebe, all of the National Security Agency (NSA). In 2002, three of the four—Binney, Loomis, and Wiebe—requested that the Department of Defense investigate why the NSA had wasted money on a multi-billion-dollar signals intelligence system called Trailblazer, which it chose instead of a significantly smaller and cheaper in-house program, ThinThread. ThinThread was widely considered to be more effective than Trailblazer.

The in-house system was jettisoned in August 2001, only weeks before 9/11, and just before it could be deployed. Wiebe later told the *Nation* that NSA intelligence had "stopped in its tracks" once the agency cancelled ThinThread.[7] The same article reported that the so-called NSA Four believed that as a result, "the agency failed to detect critical phone and e-mail communications that could have tipped U.S. intelligence to Al Qaeda's plans to attack."

Binney, Drake, Loomis, and Wiebe furthermore complained about massive corruption in the system procurement process, including bid-rigging and other forms of fraud. Moreover, while programs created for ThinThread were to be used for spying on enemy subjects, they were also used illegally for surveillance of American citizens, when earlier built-in privacy restraints were eliminated after 9/11. The four went public with this information in 2013.

In 2010, the Obama administration's Department of Justice indicted Drake on ten felony counts, including five under the

---

7   https://www.thenation.com/article/archive/obamas-crackdown-whistleblowers/

Espionage Act.[8] The charges were based primarily on information he conveyed to a *Baltimore Sun* reporter. The government alleged a mishandling of documents by Drake. If convicted, he would have faced up to thirty-five years in prison. All ten charges were dropped in 2011, when Drake pleaded guilty to the misdemeanor offense of exceeding the authorized use of a computer. For his steadfastness, Drake was awarded the Ridenhour Prize for Truth-Telling and the Sam Adams Associates for Integrity in Intelligence (SAAII) award.

After they left the NSA, Binney, Wiebe, and Loomis formed a consulting service for government agencies. But, soon enough, they discovered that they could not get any work. In 2013, the Pentagon's Inspector General rejected the trio's request for an investigation into their claims of having been blackballed.

8   https://www.smithsonianmag.com/history/leaks-and-the-law-the-story-of-thomas-drake-14796786/

Kiriakou

Ex-CIA analyst and case officer John Kiriakou is also former senior investigator for the Senate Foreign Relations Committee. He was involved in CIA counterterrorism but refused to be trained in so-called "enhanced interrogation techniques."

In 2007, after resigning from the CIA, Kiriakou gave an interview to ABC News during which he became the first former CIA officer to confirm that the agency waterboarded, and to call waterboarding torture.[9] He also revealed in the interview that it was official U.S. policy to torture prisoners.

As a result, the CIA launched an investigation into Kiriakou. In 2012, half a decade after the interview, the government charged him with five felonies. He was the sixth whistleblower indicted by the Obama administration under the Espionage Act, which had been promulgated to punish spies, not whistleblowers. Kiriakou plea bargained his way down from a potential forty-five-year sentence to one of thirty months.

As the Government Accountability Project put it: "Kiriakou is the sole CIA agent to go to jail in connection with the U.S. torture program, despite the fact that he never tortured anyone. Rather, he blew the whistle on this horrific wrongdoing."[10]

9   https://abcnews.go.com/Blotter/story?id=3978231
10   https://whistleblower.org/bio-john-kiriakou/

Associated Press

In a move to root out the source of an investigative piece on the CIA's foiling of an al-Qaeda terror plot in 2012, the Obama administration in May 2013 seized phone records from offices of the Associated Press (AP).[11] The Justice Department, with no advance warning to the AP, obtained under subpoenas records of two months' worth of the incoming and outgoing calls of approximately one hundred reporters and editors in the news organization's offices in New York, Washington, and Connecticut.

AP President and CEO Gary Pruitt protested the action in a letter to Attorney General Eric Holder, calling it a "serious interference with AP's constitutional rights to gather and report the news."[12] The records potentially revealed confidential sources and provided a road map as to how AP goes about gathering news, as well as other information that, according to Pruitt, "the government has no conceivable right to know."

The AP noted that the Obama administration had, to date, brought six cases against people suspected of leaking classified information—more than those brought by all other presidential administrations combined. The cases ranged from a CIA former officer discussing waterboarding with reporters, to a former NSA employee speaking to reporters about the "fraud, waste, and abuse" he witnessed at the agency.[13]

The Obama executive office denied any involvement in, or knowledge of, the Justice Department move, citing the supposedly insurmountable divide between the executive and judicial branches of government (although the Justice Department is part of the executive branch). Moreover, the CIA's thwarting of the plot, set to take place on the first anniversary of the White House's announcement of the killing of Osama bin Laden, contradicted the Obama administration's stance that it had no knowledge of any plans for attacks marking the anniversary.

11   https://www.theguardian.com/world/2012/may/07/cia-al-qaida-bomb-plot
12   https://www.theguardian.com/world/2013/may/14/associated-press-phone-records
13   https://www.newyorker.com/magazine/2011/05/23/the-secret-sharer

Surveillance

As a professor at Harvard Law School in 2008, Cass Sunstein wrote a controversial academic paper proposing that the U.S. government deploy teams of covert agents and pseudo-"independent" advocates to "cognitively infiltrate" online groups, websites, and activist groups that espoused what he termed "false conspiracy theories."[14] The idea was to use the agents, some of whom would be paid, to bolster citizens' trust in government officials and undermine the credibility of so-called conspiracists. The following year, Sunstein was appointed by Obama to head the Office of Information and Regulatory Affairs, a position he held for three years. The job put him in charge of policies relating to privacy, information quality, and statistical programs.

Four years later, Sunstein, a close friend of Obama's since their faculty days at the University of Chicago Law School, was named by him to serve on a five-man panel to review the National Security Agency.[15] The panel was formed in response to leaked information that was published in the *Washington Post* and the *Guardian* in June 2013 on the NSA's PRISM surveillance program, revealing the enormous breadth of its bulk spying on Americans.[16] The PRISM program was enabled by changes to U.S. surveillance law introduced under President Bush and renewed under Obama in December 2012. Classified documents had also revealed that, under the Obama administration, the NSA was collecting—indiscriminately and in bulk—the communication records of millions of U.S. citizens, regardless of whether they were suspected of any wrongdoing.

In addition to Sunstein, the review group, which Obama promised would be an "independent" and "outside" panel of experts, was made

---

14   https://papers.ssrn.com/sol3/papers.cfm?abstract_id=1084585; see also https://www.huffpost.com/entry/cass-sunsteins-thought-po_b_453562

15   https://www.theguardian.com/world/2013/aug/22/nsa-surveillance-review-panel-insiders

16   https://www.theguardian.com/world/2013/jun/06/us-tech-giants-nsa-data

up of a former deputy director of the CIA, a former member of the National Security Council, a former dean of the University of Chicago Law School, and Obama's former Chief Counselor for Privacy in the Office of Management and Budget. Director of National Intelligence James Clapper issued a memo saying he would head up the group.[17] He had recently come under fire for falsely testifying before Congress that the government did "not wittingly" collect the telephone records of millions of Americans.[18] The day after issuing the memo, however, the White House backtracked, saying Clapper's role would be limited.

The top-secret information on PRISM was leaked by former NSA contractor Edward Snowden. An internal document showed that the NSA had direct access to the systems of Google, Facebook, Apple, Microsoft, YouTube, and other major tech companies, allowing officials to collect material including search history and the content of emails, file transfers, and live chats.[19] Snowden also had leaked a court order showing that Verizon, one of America's largest telecoms providers, was handing over the calling records and telephone metadata of all its customers to the NSA on an ongoing daily basis.[20]

Just days before he left office in 2017, Obama issued new rules under Executive Order 12333 to allow the NSA to share the raw streams of communications it intercepts directly with sixteen other agencies that make up the U.S. intelligence community, including the FBI, the DEA, and the Department of Homeland Security.[21]

17   https://www.theatlantic.com/national/archive/2013/08/obamas-intelligence-chief-will-head-promised-nsa-review/312201/

18   https://www.theatlantic.com/national/archive/2013/07/clapper-letter/313691/

19   https://www.theguardian.com/world/2013/jun/06/us-tech-giants-nsa-data

20   https://www.theguardian.com/world/2013/jun/06/nsa-phone-records-verizon-court-order

21   https://theintercept.com/2017/01/13/obama-opens-nsas-vast-trove-of-warrantless-data-to-entire-intelligence-community-just-in-time-for-trump/

Snowden

While Edward Snowden took shelter in a Moscow airport after leaking embarrassing details of massive U.S. communications surveillance programs, President Obama made light of the thirty-year-old former NSA contractor as "a 29-year-old hacker."[22] In a June 29, 2013 news conference in Senegal, Obama pooh-poohed the international manhunt for Snowden, who was then wanted in the U.S. for leaking NSA documents. "I'm not going to have one case with a suspect who we're trying to extradite suddenly be elevated to the point where I've got to start doing wheeling and dealing and trading on a whole host of other issues, simply to get a guy extradited so he can face the justice system," Obama said.[23]

Two days later, however, Ecuadorean President Rafael Correa revealed that Vice President Joe Biden had placed a "cordial" telephone call to him, asking that he not grant Snowden asylum.[24] At the time, WikiLeaks founder Julian Assange had been in Ecuador's London embassy for more than a year, where he was given asylum to avoid extradition to Sweden.

In a statement issued by WikiLeaks on July 1, 2013, Snowden took issue with what he called "deception" on the part of Obama.[25] "These are the old, bad tools of political aggression. Their purpose is to frighten, not me, but those who would come after me," Snowden said. He continued:

> "For decades the United States of America has been one of the strongest defenders of the human right to seek asylum. Sadly, this right, laid out and voted for by the U.S. in Article 14 of the Universal Declaration of Human Rights, is now being rejected by the current government of

22 https://apnews.com/article/dbff8fca67a44777bc478f3de6f9873b
23 https://apnews.com/article/dbff8fca67a44777bc478f3de6f9873b
24 https://www.reuters.com/article/us-usa-security-ecuador/u-s-asked-ecuador-not-to-give-snowden-asylum-correa-idUSBRE95S0CC20130629
25 https://wikileaks.org/Statement-from-Edward-Snowden-in.html

my country. The Obama administration has now adopted the strategy of using citizenship as a weapon. Although I am convicted of nothing, it has unilaterally revoked my passport, leaving me a stateless person. Without any judicial order, the administration now seeks to stop me exercising a basic right. A right that belongs to everybody. The right to seek asylum."

Risen

New York Times reporter James Risen racked up five years fighting the Obama administration's efforts to force him to testify against a suspected whistleblower who had leaked information to him for his 2006 book, *State of War: The Secret History of the CIA and the Bush Administration.* The book included a chapter on a botched CIA plan, dating to the administration of Bill Clinton and supported by the Bush administration, to sabotage Iran's nuclear program.

Beginning in 2009, the Obama Justice Department battled for Risen, a two-time Pulitzer Prize winner, to testify at a grand jury of the suspected leaker, CIA officer Jeffrey Sterling. Risen refused to do so, and when the DOJ was rejected in court, it tried to have him testify in Sterling's trial.[26] By the summer of 2014, Risen had failed to have the Supreme Court review an order compelling him to testify about the sources in his book and he had run out of legal options.[27] In an interview with his *Times* colleague Maureen Dowd, Risen called Obama "the greatest enemy to press freedom in a generation."[28]

Among Risen's supporters were fourteen other Pulitzer Prize-winning journalists, each of whom issued statements on his behalf. "Enough is enough," wrote David Barstow, a three-time recipient.[29] "The relentless and by all appearances vindictive effort by two administrations to force Jim Risen into betraying his sources has already done substantial and lasting damage to journalism in the United States. I've felt the chill first hand. Trusted sources in Washington are scared to

26   https://www.politico.com/story/2011/05/doj-seeks-to-force-scribes-testimony-055608

27   https://www.nytimes.com/2014/06/03/us/james-risen-faces-jail-time-for-refusing-to-identify-a-confidential-source.html

28   https://www.nytimes.com/2014/08/17/opinion/sunday/maureen-dowd-wheres-the-justice-at-justice.html

29   https://rootsaction.org/statements-for-risen

talk by telephone, or by email, or even to meet for coffee, regardless of whether the subject touches on national security or not."

Late in 2014, Obama's attorney general, Eric Holder, dropped the demand that Risen reveal his sources. Soon after, Sterling was found guilty under the Espionage Act for the leak. According to the *Intercept*, "The key evidence that persuaded a jury to convict Sterling on nine felony counts consisted of phone records and emails that showed Sterling and Risen had communicated with each other. However, those records did not disclose anything about the content of their conversations."[30] The following month, Holder spoke at the National Press Club in defense of the administration's record on prosecuting leakers, saying they could have prosecuted far more than they actually did. "Simply because we have the ability to do something, should we? Members of the press have to ask the same question," Holder said.[31] "Simply because you have the ability to—because of a leaker or source of information you have—you have the ability to expose that to the public, should you? It is for you to decide, not for government to decide."

Following Holder's remarks, Trevor Timm, executive director of the Freedom of the Press Foundation, wrote:

> "The case cost Risen and his publisher an untold fortune in legal fees, dominated his life, took away from time he could've spent reporting, and likely cost the taxpayers millions of dollars. Along the way, we found out that the government had spied on virtually every aspect of James Risen's digital life, from phone calls, to emails, to credit card statements, bank records and more [. . .] Now the Justice Department wants a pat on the back. While it is unequivocally excellent news that Risen will not be forced into jail, the DOJ's behavior in this case was and still is deplorable. It has done damage to long term press freedom rights that will be very hard to undo, and the idea that this should be

30   https://theintercept.com/2018/01/19/jeffrey-sterling-cia-leaking-prison/
31   https://www.politico.com/blogs/media/2015/02/holder-dings-fox-news-in-press-club-speech-202683

looked at as a 'model' for future leak investigations is troubling, to say the least."[32]

In spite of the efforts to silence him, Risen continued to hold the powerful to account, reporting in 2015 on the "awkwardness" of Vice President Joe Biden's anti-corruption efforts.[33]

32   https://freedom.press/news/the-james-risen-case-and-eric-holders-tarnished-press-freedom-legacy/
33   https://www.nytimes.com/2015/12/09/world/europe/corruption-ukraine-joe-biden-son-hunter-biden-ties.html; also see https://theintercept.com/2019/09/25/i-wrote-about-the-bidens-and-ukraine-years-ago-then-the-right-wing-spin-machine-turned-the-story-upside-down/

Vacations

Travel expenses by Barack Obama during the eight years of his presidency came to just shy of $100 million. The $96,938,882.51 spent on travel was for family vacations, as well as politically focused trips in service of the Democratic Party and of specific candidates. This figure was based on documents obtained from the U.S. Air Force and the Secret Service under the Freedom of Information Act by the government watchdog, Judicial Watch.[34]

An example of this spendthrift attitude was Obama's April 22, 2015 Earth Day trip to the Everglades to deliver a speech on climate change. The 4.2-hour round trip to and from Miami on Air Force One cost taxpayers $866,615.40 in flight expenses alone. According to FOIA-obtained documents, Air Force One cost more than $206,000 an hour to operate. The entire trip took a total of ten hours.

Another budget-belittling jaunt was Michelle Obama's side trip to Dublin during the couple's 2013 excursion to the G-8 Conference in Belfast.[35] It is hard to imagine how the First Lady was able to spend $251,161.86 over the course of a few days' visit to the Emerald Isle. Perhaps she was hosting a leprechaun summit. The entire trip rang up a bill of $7,921,638.66.

The landmark vacation year for the Obamas was 2013, when they embarked on a Christmas sojourn to Honolulu, following a summer visit to Africa.[36] The two trips taken together incurred nearly $16 million in travel expenses alone. "The costs to taxpayers of President Obama's travel, especially his luxury vacation travel, are beyond the pale," said Judicial Watch president Tom Fitton; "and the secrecy

---

34   https://www.judicialwatch.org/press-room/press-releases/judicial-watch-new-obama-travel-costs-bring-eight-year-total-96-million/
35   https://www.judicialwatch.org/press-releases/obamas-ireland-trip/
36   https://www.judicialwatch.org/press-releases/jw-obtains-documents-revealing-high-cost-of-obama-2013-trips/

surrounding these costs shows that Obama's vows of transparency are rubbish."

The travel expenses of Vice President Joe Biden, who in 2011 was put in charge of a White House campaign to "hunt down and eliminate misspent tax dollars in every agency and department across the Federal Government," were likewise an immense burden on taxpayers.[37] A 2012 report estimated that $1 million was spent annually on simply shuttling Biden to and from his home state of Delaware every weekend.[38]

37 https://obamawhitehouse.archives.gov/goodgovernment/actions/campaign-cut-waste
38 https://www.newsmax.com/Newsfront/Biden-weekend-travel-Air-Force-Two/2012/06/04/id/441168/; https://www.syracuse.com/news/2014/07/did_taxpayers_pick_up_the_bill_for_vp_joe_bidens_trip_to_auburn_wedding.html

Clinton Endorsement

White House Chief of Staff Denis McDonough announced in January 2016 that no Democratic candidate would get President Obama's endorsement until the candidate had earned the party's nomination. "We'll do exactly what has been done in the past, which is when the nominee will be set, then the president will be out there [for him/her]," McDonough said on NBC's *Meet the Press*.[39]

But on June 9 of that year, six weeks prior to the nomination of Hillary Clinton at the Democratic National Convention, Obama—after meeting with Clinton rival Bernie Sanders—formally endorsed Clinton as his party's nominee for the 2016 presidential election. In a phone interview with *Politico* the day she received the endorsement, Clinton expressed her gratitude, noting that Obama "has been very supportive to me throughout this campaign."[40]

39   https://www.nbcnews.com/meet-the-press/pres-obama-won-t-make-dem-primary-endorsement-wh-n493606

40   https://www.politico.com/story/2016/06/president-obama-endorses-hillary-clinton-224130

Trans-Pacific Partnership

The Trans-Pacific Partnership (TPP) agreement was a multilateral free-trade treaty negotiated by twelve Pacific Rim nations: the United States, Australia, Brunei, Canada, Chile, Japan, Malaysia, Mexico, New Zealand, Peru, Singapore, and Vietnam. It contained measures to lower both non-tariff and tariff barriers to trade and establish an investor state dispute settlement mechanism.

Following five years of negotiations, the twelve countries signed the deal on February 4, 2016, the first step toward a hoped-for ratification. Outside the signing ceremony in New Zealand, more than one thousand protesters disrupted traffic. "There is wide spread grassroots opposition to the TPP in many countries," Reuters reported at the time.[41] "Opponents have criticized the secrecy surrounding TPP talks, raised concerns about reduced access to things like affordable medicines, and a clause which allows foreign investors the right to sue if they feel their profits have been impacted by a law or policy in the host country." Labor groups opposed the pact, fearful it would move U.S. jobs to lower-income countries. Environmentalists fought against it, charging it would give corporations special rights to run roughshod over trees, fish, and wildlife.[42]

On January 23, 2017, Donald Trump signed a presidential memorandum to withdraw the U.S. from the TPP, after saying the agreement would undermine the U.S. economy and its independence. Among those applauding the move was Senator Bernie Sanders, who had stood with U.S. labor unions in opposition to the TPP. "For the last 30 years, we have had a series of trade deals ... which have cost us millions of

---

41   https://www.reuters.com/article/us-trade-tpp/trans-pacific-partnership-trade-deal-signed-but-years-of-negotiations-still-to-come-idUSKCN0VD08S

42   https://stopthetpp.org/we-live-in-one-world-the-trans-pacific-partnership-and-the-environment/

decent-paying jobs and caused a 'race to the bottom' which has low-ered wages for American workers," Sanders said in a statement.[43]

The U.S. withdrawal from the TPP marked a defeat for former president Obama, as well as vice president Biden, both of whom had pushed hard for it. In Mexico in early 2015, Biden called the proposed deal "a game changer," describing it as a "comprehensive, high-stand-ard trade agreement" that would raise the bar for 21st century trade.[44] In October 2015, shortly after the negotiating countries had announced their agreement on the deal, Obama used his weekly address to defend the TPP: "Those who oppose passing this new trade deal are really just accepting a status quo that everyone knows puts us at a disadvantage."[45]

What everyone knew, however, was little. Except for parts of the deal that were leaked, the public was kept in the dark on what exactly the deal constituted. Negotiations among the twelve nations' repre-sentatives were conducted behind closed doors. Members of the U.S. Congress were allowed to view only selected portions of the docu-ments under supervision.

"In the coming weeks and months, you'll be able to read every word of this agreement online well before I sign it," Obama said in his October 2015 address, deflecting any secrecy criticisms.

Almost two years earlier, in November 2013, WikiLeaks released the draft text of the TPP's chapter on intellectual property rights.[46] Following the leak, the *Guardian* reported:

> "The 30,000-word intellectual property chapter contains proposals
> to increase the term of patents, including medical patents, beyond
> 20 years, and lower global standards for patentability. It also pushes

43   https://www.washingtonpost.com/news/powerpost/wp/2017/01/23/sanders-praises-trump-for-nixing-tpp-delighted-to-work-with-him-on-pro-worker-policies/

44   https://www.cbsnews.com/news/biden-supports-trade-deal-despite-opposition-from-unions/

45   https://www.theguardian.com/business/2015/oct/10/obama-defends-tpp-deal-dismisses-secrecy-concerns

46   https://wikileaks.org/tpp/pressrelease.html

for aggressive measures to prevent hackers breaking copyright protection, although that comes with some exceptions: protection can be broken in the course of 'lawfully authorised activities carried out by government employees, agents, or contractors for the purpose of law enforcement, intelligence, essential security, or similar governmental purposes.'"[47]

WikiLeaks founder Julian Assange put things more succinctly:

"The U.S. administration is aggressively pushing the TPP through the U.S. legislative process on the sly. If instituted, the TPP's intellectual property regime would trample over individual rights and free expression, as well as ride roughshod over the intellectual and creative commons. If you read, write, publish, think, listen, dance, sing or invent; if you farm or consume food; if you're ill now or might one day be ill, the TPP has you in its crosshairs."[48]

In response to the WikiLeaks release, as well as an earlier leak of the TPP's investor–state dispute resolution proposals and "numerous reports in the business press," Nobel-winning economist Joseph E. Stiglitz wrote an open letter to TPP negotiators.[49] Asserting that the agreement "presents grave risks on all sort of topics," Stiglitz, a professor of finance and economics at the Columbia Business School, urged the negotiators to resist a number of the TPP's intellectual property provisions, and railed against the secrecy measures.

"The decision to make the negotiating text secret from the public (even though the details are accessible to hundreds of advisors to big corporations) makes it difficult for the public to offer informed commentary," Stiglitz wrote in the December 6, 2013 letter. "The TPP proposes to freeze into a binding trade agreement many of the worst features of the worst laws in the TPP countries, making needed reforms

---

47   https://www.theguardian.com/media/2013/nov/13/wikileaks-trans-pacific-partnership-chapter-secret
48   https://wikileaks.org/tpp/pressrelease.html
49   https://www.keionline.org/sites/default/files/jstiglitzTPP.pdf

extremely difficult if not impossible. The investor state dispute resolution mechanisms should not be shrouded in mystery to the general public, while the same provisions are routinely discussed with advisors to big corporations."

The eleven remaining nations negotiated a new trade agreement called the Comprehensive and Progressive Agreement for Trans-Pacific Partnership. It incorporates most of the provisions of the TPP and came into force on December 30, 2018.

Japan

Edward Snowden, who in 2013 disclosed vast governmental surveillance in the United States, warned in June 2016 that everyone in Japan was being subjected to similar surveillance, likewise initiated by the U.S. government.[50]

Snowden had lived in Japan from 2009 to 2011, while he was a contractor to the National Security Agency through computer giant Dell. He worked on a surveillance program at Yokota, an American air base near Tokyo.

Snowden made the statement via videoconference from Russia, and it was broadcast to a symposium focusing on surveillance in contemporary society at the University of Tokyo. He stressed that all data inputted via mobile phone or computer in Japan could be legally collected by the U.S. intelligence agency.

Snowden noted that the 2013 enactment of a controversial law, the Act on the Protection of Specially Designated Secrets, allowed Japanese public agencies wide discretion in classifying defense, military, counterterrorism, and diplomatic information as state secrets, and provided strict penalties for leakers, including up to ten years in prison. In the weekly Japanese journal *Sunday Mainichi*, Snowden said the law was designed and implemented by the U.S. government to facilitate the NSA's undercover activities in Japan with the Japanese prime minister's encouragement.

Classified NSA documents leaked by Snowden in 2017 revealed more details concerning the complex relationship between Japan and the NSA over a period of more than six decades. The documents, reported the *Intercept*, confirmed that "Japan has allowed NSA to maintain at least three bases on its territory and contributed more than half a billion dollars to help finance the NSA's facilities and operations. In

---

50   https://www.japantimes.co.jp/news/2016/06/04/national/nsa-whistleblower-snowden-says-u-s-government-carrying-out-mass-surveillance-in-japan/

return, NSA has kitted out Japanese spies with powerful surveillance tools and shared intelligence with them."[51] However, the report noted, "there is a duplicitous dimension to the partnership. While the NSA has maintained friendly ties with its Japanese counterparts and benefited from their financial generosity, at the same time it has secretly spied on Japanese officials and institutions."

51 https://theintercept.com/2017/04/24/japans-secret-deals-with-the-nsa-that-expand-global-surveillance/

Democracy Rankings

The Democracy Ranking is an index created by the Democracy Ranking Association in Vienna. It is an annual ranking of all country-based democracies in the world that focuses on "the quality of democracy in an international perspective." In 2016, Obama's last year in office, the top twenty countries in order of ranking were:[52]

1. Norway
2. Switzerland
3. Sweden
4. Finland
5. Denmark
6. Netherlands
7. New Zealand
8. Germany
9. Ireland
10. Australia
11. Belgium
12. Canada
13. Austria
14. United Kingdom
15. France
16. United States
17. Slovenia
18. Japan
19. Spain
20. Portugal

The United States' 16th place reflected a drop of one place from 2011, when it ranked 15th.[53]

52   http://democracyranking.org/wordpress/rank/democracy-ranking-2016/
53   http://www.democracyranking.org/downloads/Key-findings_Democracy-Ranking_2011_en-A4.pdf

Expense Accounts

In July 2016, less than six months before he became a former president, Obama vetoed a measure that would have capped the taxpayer-funded expense accounts given to former presidents at $200,000 a year.[54] The work-related expense accounts cover costs for travel, staff, and office maintenance, for the remainder of a former president's lifetime. This is additional to the pension received by former presidents which, for calendar year 2016, was $205,700.[55] Obama said in a message to Congress that he was vetoing the bill because if the allowances were capped, some former presidents would have to lay-off staff, cancel leases, or return office furniture. The most recent former president at the time, George W. Bush, had received $1,098,000 for pension and benefit costs in 2015.[56]

54   https://eu.usatoday.com/story/news/politics/2016/07/22/obama-vetoes-cuts-former-presidents-expense-accounts/87462850/
55   https://fas.org/sgp/crs/misc/RL34631.pdf
56   https://fas.org/sgp/crs/misc/RL34631.pdf

Democratic Party

For the Democratic Party, the Obama years began on a high note. Along with Obama's own victory, the Democrats won a trifecta of sorts, having gained majority status in both chambers of Congress, as well as a majority of state legislatures and governorships.

At the beginning of the 111th Congress, in January 2009, Democrats held a majority 57 seats (of 100 total) in the Senate and a majority 257 seats (of 435 total) in the House. By contrast, at the start of the 115th Congress in January 2017, eight years into the Obama presidency and with Trump's presidential victory freshly at hand, the Democrats held a minority 46 seats in the Senate, and a minority 194 seats in the House. In eight years under Obama, the Democratic Party lost 11 seats in the Senate, losing its upper hand in the process. During that same eight-year period, they also lost 63 seats in the House, as well as their dominance.

Much the same thing happened at the state level. In 2009, 28 states had Democratic governors. By 2017, that number had dropped to 16. Twenty-seven of 49 state legislatures (Nebraska has a unicameral; all other states have two legislative chambers) had a Democratic majority in 2009. In 2017, that number had been whittled down to 14, almost half the number from eight years earlier.

The media was harsh on Obama. A *Washington Post* headline a year after his departure from the White House read: "The Democrats Got Rolled. They Can Thank Barack Obama."[57] Even NPR was brutal, headlining a piece prior to the 2016 election: "The Democratic Party Got Crushed During the Obama Presidency."[58] Vice President Joe Biden shouldered some blame as well. In a 2017 CNBC commentary,

---

57   https://www.washingtonpost.com/opinions/democrats-just-got-rolled-they-can-blame-barack-obama/2018/01/22/60c8be48-ffaa-11e7-8acf-ad2991367d9d_story.html

58   https://www.npr.org/2016/03/04/469052020/the-democratic-party-got-crushed-during-the-obama-presidency-heres-why

he was called "the exact opposite of the kind of candidate voters in both parties proved they want in the 2016 election."[59] While Obama was not judged the sole culprit in this multi-year rout, he still figured prominently. Democratic leaders repeatedly referred to him as aloof and fundamentally disinterested in bolstering the party's chances of winning.[60]

59   https://www.cnbc.com/2017/11/13/joe-biden-will-never-be-president-democrats-
      must-end-the-madness-commentary.html
60   https://www.theatlantic.com/politics/archive/2013/02/congressional-democrats-are-
      angry-at-obama-again/272844/

Freedom of the Press

Upon ending his tenure as commander in chief in January 2017, Obama delivered a send-off to the White House press corps that was rich in flattery, exuberantly pointing out its importance to America and our democracy.[61] "You're supposed to cast a critical eye on folks who hold enormous power," Obama said. "Having you in this building has made this place work better. It keeps us honest, makes us work harder."

At the time, the United States was listed 41st out of 180 countries in the 2016 World Press Freedom Index, one place above Slovenia and one below Burkina Faso. The annual rankings evaluate pluralism, independence of the media, quality of legislative framework, and safety of journalists and are published by Reporters Without Borders, a non-profit group dedicated to protecting journalists and their freedom of expression.[62]

America's place on the list had fallen precipitously since Obama took office. In 2009, the U.S. was ranked 20th out of 175 countries, tied with the United Kingdom and Luxembourg. That was up from 2008 when the U.S. came in at 36th place among 173 countries, a ranking shared with Bosnia and Herzegovina, Cape Verde, South Africa, Spain, and Taiwan. (The number of countries in the rankings varies somewhat from year to year.)

By 2015, the U.S. had dropped to 49th on that year's list of 179 countries, squeezed in between Malta and Comoros. In a statement on World Press Freedom Day of that year, Obama reaffirmed the "vital role" of a free press: "Journalists give all of us, as citizens, the chance to know the truth about our countries, ourselves, our governments. That makes us better, it makes us stronger, it gives voice to the voiceless, exposes injustice, and holds leaders like me accountable."[63]

61 https://time.com/4638565/donald-trump-press-access/
62 https://rsf.org/en/world-press-freedom-index
63 https://obamawhitehouse.archives.gov/the-press-office/2015/05/01/remarks-president-world-press-freedom-day

Speeches

In 2017, former president Barack Obama made three speeches for $400,000 each to Wall Street firms Cantor Fitzgerald, the Carlyle Group, and Northern Trust Corp.[64]

As *Vox* stated:

"Former President Barack Obama's decision to accept a $400,000 fee to speak at a health care conference organized by the bond firm Cantor Fitzgerald is easily understood. That's so much cash, for so little work, that it would be extraordinarily difficult for anyone to turn it down. And the precedent established by former Presidents Bill Clinton and George W. Bush, to say nothing of former Federal Reserve Chairs Ben Bernanke and Alan Greenspan and a slew of other high-ranking former officials, is that there is nothing wrong with taking the money. Indeed, to not take the money might be a problem for someone in Obama's position. It would set a precedent. Obama would be suggesting that for an economically comfortable high-ranking former government official to be out there doing paid speaking gigs would be corrupt, sleazy, or both. He'd be looking down his nose at the other corrupt, sleazy former high-ranking government officials and making enemies. Which is exactly why he should have turned down the gig."[65]

For each of these three speeches, Obama received the equivalent of his annual salary as president and more than seven times the then median income of American families.[66] This earned him a position among the top ten highest paid public speakers in the U.S. He went on to deliver an estimated fifty paid speeches a year in 2017 and 2018, and as recently as May 2019 was paid to speak at the EXMA conference in Bogotá,

---

64   https://www.independent.co.uk/news/world/americas/us-politics/barack-obama-speeches-fee-wall-street-latest-a7954156.html
65   https://www.vox.com/policy-and-politics/2017/4/25/15419740/obama-speaking-fee
66   https://www.nytimes.com/2017/04/27/opinion/400000-for-one-speech-for-ex-presidents-it-is-now-the-norm.html

Colombia, a country in which his reported $600,000 fee was seventy-two times the average worker's income.[67]

Joe Biden also engaged in lucrative speaking arrangements in the years following his vice presidency. The self-described "Middle Class Joe" earned $15.6 million in the two years after he left office, the majority from book payments and speaking fees.[68]

67   https://www.wsws.org/en/articles/2019/06/20/obam-j20.html
68   https://edition.cnn.com/2019/07/09/politics/joe-biden-tax-returns/index.html

Real Estate

In late 2019, a nominee trust representing the former First Family completed the purchase of a Martha's Vineyard house that cost $11.75 million. Sitting on nearly 30 acres, the Obamas' house is nearly 7,000 square feet. The seller was private equity investor and owner of the Boston Celtics, Wycliffe Grousbeck.

Former vice president Joe Biden purchased a $2.7 million, 4,800-square-foot vacation house in 2017 to supplement his nearly 7,000-square-foot lakeside home in Delaware. In the run up to the 2020 presidential election, the *Washington Post* reported that Biden was renting a 12,000-square-foot, 5 bedroom house from a well-connected, politically active donor.[69] Biden's campaign declined to disclose details about the financial provisions for the house.

---

69   https://www.washingtonpost.com/politics/joe-biden-earned-156-million-in-the-two-years-after-leaving-the-vice-presidency/2019/07/09/55aad492-a27e-11e9-b8c8-75dae2607e60_story.html

Sanders Endorsement

Former president Barack Obama took a neutral public position on the 2020 Democratic presidential primary, even telling a crowd at a November 2019 Democracy Alliance conference: "Look, we have a field of very accomplished, very serious and passionate and smart people who have a history of public service, and whoever emerges from the primary process, I will work my tail off to make sure that they are the next president."[70]

The possible exception may have been Bernie Sanders. According to *Politico* later that month: "Back when Sanders seemed like more of a threat than he does now, Obama said privately that if Bernie were running away with the nomination, Obama would speak up to stop him."[71]

In December 2019, the *Hill* reported that Obama had voiced his support for Senator Elizabeth Warren during behind-the-scenes sessions with donors.[72] "The former president has stopped short of an endorsement of Warren in these conversations and has emphasized that he is not endorsing in the Democratic primary race," according to the report. "But he also has vouched for her credentials, making it clear in these private sessions that he deems her a capable candidate and potential president, sources say."

The following April, less than a week after Sanders dropped out of the race, Obama threw his support behind the former vice president in a twelve-minute video. "Joe has the character and the experience to guide us through one of our darkest times and heal us through a long recovery," Obama said.[73]

---

70 https://www.huffingtonpost.co.uk/entry/obama-bernie-sanders-2020-nomination_n_5ddd31a1e4b00149f724793b

71 https://www.politico.com/news/magazine/2019/11/26/barack-obama-2020-democrats-candidates-biden-073025

72 https://thehill.com/homenews/administration/475576-obama-talks-up-warren-behind-closed-doors-to-wealthy-donors

73 https://www.theguardian.com/us-news/2020/apr/14/barack-obama-endorse-joe-biden-2020-election-democrats

PART II

ENVIRONMENT

Cap and Trade

In the summer of 2010, President Obama pushed for the passage of a cap-and-trade bill, the American Clean Energy and Security Act. This would set a nationwide limit on carbon dioxide emissions and allow companies to buy and sell permits to pollute. Therefore, a company could create more greenhouse gases than would otherwise be permitted, provided they purchased credits from other companies that had a surplus of credits because they produced less greenhouse gases than expected. This seemingly reasonable proposal targeting climate change, wrote Elaine Kamarck of the Brookings Institution, "failed miserably."[74] It then "fell off the political radar," according to Princeton professor Meg Jacobs.

The cap-and-trade bill was actually introduced in the House a year earlier in May 2009, and it passed the next month by a narrow vote of 219–212.[75] This was the first time Congress approved a bill aimed at curbing greenhouse gas emissions.[76] But following its victory in the House, the bill languished in the Senate for over a year. Then, as a result of interim elections in November 2010, the Republicans took back their majority in the House, while increasing their presence in the Senate. It was "curtains" for this sensible environmental innovation.

74 https://bostonreview.net/politics/elaine-kamarck-fragile-legacy-barack-obama
75 https://www.theguardian.com/environment/2009/jun/27/barack-obama-climate-change-bill
76 https://www.nytimes.com/2009/06/27/us/politics/27climate.html

Arctic

In his first presidential campaign, Obama made it clear that climate change was a top national priority. But in direct contradiction to his 2008 campaign pledge to put an end to Arctic offshore exploratory drilling, in March 2010 Obama opened the northern coast of Alaska to exploratory drilling for oil and gas, claiming it to be a good means of stimulating the local economy.[77]

Finally, in December 2016, with exactly a month left in office, Obama banned oil and gas drilling in nearly all the waters comprising the Arctic Ocean. This did not halt the use of pre-existing oil wells and, at the time, oil industry spokespeople stated that the incoming president would find a way to reverse the decision. Sure enough, in April 2017, President Trump issued an executive order reversing the bans—a move that was later found to be unlawful by an Alaska judge.[78]

77   https://www.theguardian.com/world/2010/mar/31/barack-obama-drilling-offshore-approves

78   https://www.theguardian.com/environment/2019/mar/30/alaska-judge-blocks-trump-arctic-atlantic-drilling

Oceans

In the wake of the 2010 Deepwater Horizon explosion and oil spill, President Obama issued Executive Order 13547, creating, for the first time, a National Ocean Policy. The order emphasized that Deepwater was "a stark reminder of how vulnerable our marine environments are, and how much communities and the nation rely on healthy and resilient ocean and coastal ecosystems."[79] It stated its goal of achieving an America "whose stewardship ensures that the ocean, our coasts, and the Great Lakes are healthy and resilient, safe and productive, and understood and treasured so as to promote the well-being, prosperity, and security of present and future generations."

On June 19, 2018, President Trump issued Executive Order 13840, replacing the Obama policy with a new policy order that neglected to mention the Deepwater disaster, zeroing in instead on "the economy, security, global competitiveness," as well as a need for streamlining the Obama policy.[80] It relied on states to take the political initiative in ocean issues. Moreover, it deemphasized the need—indeed, it eliminated the requirement—for indigenous group representation in decision-making. This was true even if, or perhaps especially if, an indigenous group obtains its livelihood from the ocean. Trump's executive order was widely seen, by detractors and proponents alike, as a move away from focusing on the environment and stewardship thereof, to matters solely concerned with the economy and the extraction of natural resources.

---

79   https://obamawhitehouse.archives.gov/the-press-office/executive-order-
     stewardship-ocean-our-coasts-and-great-lakes
80   https://www.federalregister.gov/documents/2018/06/22/2018-13640/ocean-policy-
     to-advance-the-economic-security-and-environmental-interests-of-the-united-
     states; https://www.whitehouse.gov/briefings-statements/president-donald-j-trump-
     promoting-americas-ocean-economy/

Nuclear Energy

As he stated in a February 2012 speech, Obama was proud of having "supported the first nuclear power plant in three decades."[81] He was referring to the two nuclear reactors that had just been licensed for construction at Southern Nuclear Operating Company's Vogtle site south of Augusta, for which his administration provided $8.3 billion in loan guarantees. At the time, a Gallup poll showed a bare majority, 52 percent, of Democrats supporting nuclear power.[82]

By 2016, according to another Gallup poll, a mere 34 percent of Democrats were behind nuclear energy—support had plunged 18 percent in four years. The president's outward enthusiasm for this potentially catastrophic type of energy declined accordingly. However, as late as November 2015, the Obama administration held a nuclear energy summit at the White House at which it was announced that it would supplement its existing $12.5 billion loan guarantee program to build new nuclear reactors.[83]

81 https://www.politifact.com/factchecks/2012/mar/02/barack-obama/obama-says-he-supported-first-nuclear-power-plant-/

82 https://news.gallup.com/poll/190064/first-time-majority-oppose-nuclear-energy.aspx

83 https://obamawhitehouse.archives.gov/the-press-office/2015/11/06/fact-sheet-obama-administration-announces-actions-ensure-nuclear-energy

Flint

Soon after Flint, Michigan switched its water source to the Flint River in April 2014, residents began to complain that the water tasted and smelled strange. The following year, a leaked internal Environmental Protection Agency (EPA) memo expressed concern over alarmingly high and dangerous levels of lead in Flint's water supply.[84]

In his film *Fahrenheit 9/11*, Michael Moore condemned President Obama for indecisiveness during the Flint water crisis as well as his initial failure to federalize, which would have engendered a more efficient, coordinated response at a far earlier stage. The people of Flint relied on bottled water until early 2018, when the state supply ran out.

It wasn't until January 2016, nearly two years into the mess, that the Obama EPA issued a federal emergency order. Three months later, the president finally traveled to Flint for "briefings." Only two months prior to his trip, EPA administrator Gina McCarthy had testified before Congress that she had known residents of Flint were exposed to poisonous water several months before the agency took action.

Why did Obama delay in ordering McCarthy to use her congressionally mandated emergency powers under the Safe Drinking Water Act? As per SDWA section 1431:

> Upon receipt of information that a contaminant that is present in or likely to enter a public water system or an underground source of drinking water [. . .] that may present an imminent and substantial endangerment to the health of persons, the EPA Administrator may take any action she deems necessary to protect human health.

Visiting Flint in May 2016, Obama failed to explain the delay, focusing instead on the fact that the federal response was now underway. Speaking to a crowd in a high school gymnasium, he promised free water and filters, expanded Medicaid for children who may have been

---

84   http://mediad.publicbroadcasting.net/p/michigan/files/201602/Miguels-Memo.pdf

exposed, and job training programs. He called the crisis a preventable "man-made disaster" which he said was caused by disinvestment in poor communities.[85] During a coughing fit, he asked for a glass of water. "I really did need a glass of water," he said. "This is not a stunt. If you're using a filter, if you're installing it, then Flint water at this point is drinkable."

85   https://www.usatoday.com/story/news/politics/2016/05/04/obama-flint-visit-drinking-water-lead-poisoning/83916778/

Air Pollution

In August 2015 the Obama administration launched a major response to global warming. Dubbed the Clean Power Plan (CPP) and weighing in at 460 pages, its goal was to lower carbon dioxide emissions from power plants by 32 percent by the year 2030, relative to a 2005 baseline.[86] The plan encouraged the use of renewable energy in place of other energy sources, particularly coal.

Many environmental groups characterized the plan as too little, too late. Greenpeace described the new rules as "an important step forward" but "woefully inadequate on its own."[87] Indeed, the plan, focusing on power plant pollution, would result in a rather tepid 6 percent reduction in greenhouse gas emissions nationally.[88] According to the Union of Concerned Scientists, under one scenario, "the world's industrialized nations will have to reduce their emissions an average of 70 to 80 percent below 2000 levels by 2050," in order to keep the global temperature from rising 2°C relative to a baseline at the beginning of the Industrial Revolution.[89] As of March 2020, the global temperature was 1.16°C above the baseline and the second highest in the 141-year record.

Despite the Obama administration's somewhat modest aspirations, in 2017 President Trump directed the Environmental Protection Agency (EPA) to review the CPP, as well as withdrawing the United States from the Paris Agreement. The Clean Power Plan was scrapped in June 2019 and replaced with the Affordable Clean Energy rule (ACE), a move which has provoked opposition from environmental groups and a lawsuit against the EPA brought by twenty-two states.

---

86   https://obamawhitehouse.archives.gov/the-press-office/2015/08/03/fact-sheet-president-obama-announce-historic-carbon-pollution-standards
87   https://www.greenpeace.org/usa/news/calling-on-the-obama-administration-for-a-real-solution-to-climate-change/
88   https://www.vox.com/2015/8/2/9086559/obama-climate-plan-preview
89   https://www.ucsusa.org/resources/target-us-emissions-reductions

Another environmental forward step of the Obama administration was in the crosshairs of Trump's EPA in recent years. This concerns a series of regulations governing a harsh pollutant, coal ash, the major byproduct of coal-burning power plants. In December 2008, a storage pond in Kingston, Tennessee ruptured, releasing a cascade of 5.4 million cubic yards of coal-ash sludge that polluted the Emory River and damaged nearby homes and property. Then, in 2014, another disastrous spill occurred in North Carolina when an underground drainage pipe burst at a Duke Energy coal-ash storage site, causing 39,000 tons of toxic ash to spew into the Dan River.

In response to these spills, the Obama EPA revised design standards and monitoring systems for coal ash storage in order to protect groundwater, with regulations put into effect in 2015.[90] But fewer than three years after the rules were effectuated, the Trump administration proposed a major revision that would give states and utilities more leeway in determining how coal ash is stored, as well as whether groundwater monitoring is necessary.[91] Bridget Lee, a staff attorney with the Sierra Club, said the Trump proposals were "hard to see as anything other than a giveaway to a polluter."[92] In July 2020, the EPA finalized an action extending the life of coal ash pits which, under the Obama regulations, would've had to close by 2021. According to Earthjustice attorney Lisa Evans, "this rule allows tens of millions of tons of additional toxic waste to be placed in impoundments we know are leaking."[93]

Perhaps the most important Obama-era air pollution innovation was the Corporate Average Fuel Economy (CAFE) measure. Finalized in 2012, CAFE would have required car manufacturers to increase

---

90   https://www.epa.gov/coalash/coal-ash-rule
91   https://eu.usatoday.com/story/news/politics/2018/03/06/environmentalists-accuse-epa-gutting-obama-era-safeguards-coal-ash-disposal/399351002/
92   https://eu.usatoday.com/story/news/politics/2018/03/06/environmentalists-accuse-epa-gutting-obama-era-safeguards-coal-ash-disposal/399351002/
93   https://thehill.com/policy/energy-environment/509792-epa-rule-extends-life-of-toxic-coal-ash-ponds

the fuel efficiency of new cars and trucks from an average of 35 miles per gallon to between 50 and 52.6 miles per gallon by 2025, revised from the initial goal of 54.5 mpg.[94] The reduction in pollution due to greater fuel economy would be somewhat offset by increased driving as a result of cheaper fuel. Nevertheless, the plan was expected to dramatically reduce U.S. oil consumption and greenhouse gas emissions.

Even this modest decrease was too much to take for the Trump administration, which announced in April 2018 that the mileage goals "are not appropriate and should be revised."[95] In August of that year, in a statement titled "Make Cars Great Again", the EPA presented a plan to freeze mile-per-gallon standards for cars and light trucks after the 2020 model year, claiming this would benefit the consumer by keeping car prices down. Trump also claimed the proposal would make cars "substantially safer", despite an internal EPA email showing that the revision was expected to increase highway deaths.[96]

The Trump administration moved to revoke three of Obama's boldest environmental innovations within its first two years. This regressive U-turn on the environment seemed all but inevitable. Perhaps Trump's successor will prove to be less predictable.

94   https://obamawhitehouse.archives.gov/the-press-office/2012/08/28/obama-administration-finalizes-historic-545-MPG-fuel-efficiency-standard

95   https://archive.epa.gov/epa/newsreleases/epa-administrator-pruitt-ghg-emissions-standards-cars-and-light-trucks-should-be.html

96   https://www.vox.com/2019/8/21/20826601/trump-auto-company-fuel-economy-california

Flood Standards

On August 15, 2017, President Trump rolled back an Obama order intended to stop federally funded infrastructure projects from going forward unless they met "flooding resilience" standards.[97] Under Obama's 2015 executive order, which had yet to be implemented, infrastructure projects like roads and bridges would have to be designed to withstand rising sea levels and other consequences of "climate change and other threats."[98]

Obama's flood risk reduction standard ostensibly would have had a spillover effect on the construction industry in general. Barely having had a chance to be implemented, it was instead eliminated.

97 https://www.newsweek.com/trump-signed-away-obamas-flood-risk-rules-weeks-hurricane-harvey-hit-655712
98 https://obamawhitehouse.archives.gov/the-press-office/2015/01/30/executive-order-establishing-federal-flood-risk-management-standard-and-

Bees

In 2015, the Obama White House announced a plan to stanch the precipitous decline in the U.S. bee population that had taken place in recent decades. Bee loss is measured from year to year, and from April 2014 to April 2015, 40.6 percent of honey bee colonies died.[99] An acceptable level of loss for that year, according to scientists, was closer to 18 percent. This was also the first time in history that there were more bee deaths over the summer than the winter. The following year—2015 to 2016—had similarly high losses, at 40.5 percent.

The Obama plan included planting pollinator-friendly landscaping around federal buildings. What it conspicuously left out was the banning of neonicotinoids, powerful pesticides widely implicated as being a major factor in the bees' alarming decline. Neonicotinoids were identified as being firmly linked to mass die-offs of bees as early as 2013.[100] Obama banned their use in National Wildlife Refuges in 2014, but failed to implement widespread bans during his two terms. Peter Jenkins, attorney with the Center for Food Safety, noted that the 2015 plan evaded the question of restricting neonicotinoids "by calling for more research, as it does in many areas. Pollinators cannot wait for more research."[101]

The Trump administration reversed the ban of neonicotinoids in wildlife refuges in 2018, and in 2019 the EPA granted "emergency" permissions for use of the insecticide sulfoxaflor, considered highly

99   https://beeinformed.org/citizen-science/loss-and-management-survey/
100   https://www.efsa.europa.eu/en/press/news/130116; also see https://www.theguardian.com/environment/2014/may/09/honeybees-dying-insecticide-harvard-study
101   https://www.centerforfoodsafety.org/healthy-home/3274/healthy-home/press-releases/3929/white-house-plan-to-protect-pollinators-aims-high-but-falls-short-on-deliverables

toxic to bees, on 16 million acres of crops.[102] In February 2020, the EPA enabled the continued use of five neonicotinoid pesticides known to be harmful to bees.[103] Annual honey bee losses remained above 40 percent in four of the last five years, and 2018–2019 saw the highest winter losses on record.

102   https://www.theguardian.com/environment/2018/aug/04/trump-administration-lifts-ban-on-pesticides-linked-to-declining-bee-numbers;https://www.federalregister.gov/documents/2019/02/14/2019-02354/pesticide-emergency-exemptions-agency-decisions-and-state-and-federal-agency-crisis-declarations
103   https://www.nrdc.org/media/2020/200130

Monarch Butterflies

The monarch butterfly population in the U.S. was 78 percent lower in 2016 than it was in the mid-1990s. Monarch populations hit record lows in both 2013 and 2014, while 2015 and 2016 saw little improvement. According to the Center for Biological Diversity:

> "The butterfly's dramatic decline has been driven in large part by the widespread planting of genetically engineered crops in the Midwest, where most monarchs are born. The vast majority of genetically engineered crops are made to be resistant to Monsanto's Roundup herbicide, which is a potent killer of milkweed, the monarch caterpillar's only food source. The dramatic surge in Roundup use and 'Roundup Ready' crops has virtually wiped out milkweed plants in midwestern corn and soybean fields."[104]

Addressing the crisis, the Obama White House issued a statement in June 2016 that included the following:

> "Consider carefully how you wish to manage your land—green and manicured but with few species, or a little scruffy yet rich with life? Pesticides have empowered us to efficiently kill unwanted plants and insects but a pest to you may be a home to a pollinator, and inappropriate application may cause collateral damage to beneficial plants or insects. If and when we need to use these chemical tools, we should do so with wisdom and reflection."[105]

In 2015, Obama proposed a $3.2 million expenditure for the creation of a butterfly "corridor" along Interstate Highway 35. It is not known whether this was implemented.

In 2016, two conservation groups filed a lawsuit against the Obama administration for its failure to protect the monarch butterfly

---

104   https://www.biologicaldiversity.org/news/press_releases/2016/monarch-butterfly-03-10-2016.html
105   https://obamawhitehouse.archives.gov/blog/2016/06/22/bees-butterflies-and-you

under the Endangered Species Act.[106] This followed a 2014 petition filed by the groups for the U.S. Fish and Wildlife Service to protect the monarch as a "threatened species" following a 90 percent population decline over the preceding two decades. The Service failed to reach a decision within the allotted timeframe of twelve months, prompting the lawsuit. As of October 2020, a decision has not been issued. Meanwhile, the milkweed-destroying Roundup is still used copiously and monarch populations have plunged to well below the extinction threshold estimated by scientists.[107]

106 https://www.biologicaldiversity.org/news/press_releases/2016/monarch-butterfly-03-10-2016.html

107 https://www.biologicaldiversity.org/species/invertebrates/monarch_butterfly/monarch-population-2020.html

Dakota Access Pipeline

President Obama successfully blocked the construction of a disputed segment of the Dakota Access Pipeline one month before he left office. This was a clear victory for environmentalists and Native Americans, and it was not the first time the Obama administration had come down in favor of opponents of this major pipeline and its predecessor, the Keystone XL, which Obama thwarted in 2015.[108]

However, this progressive act on Obama's part would not be upheld so as to become part of his legacy. On January 24, 2017, newly elected President Trump cleared the way for the construction of the Dakota Access and Keystone XL oil pipelines.[109] The former was completed in April 2017, while the latter remains unfinished due to a lengthy environmental review process that could jeopardize the project's existence.[110]

108   https://www.theguardian.com/environment/2015/feb/24/obama-vetoes-keystone-xl-pipeline-bill

109   https://www.theguardian.com/us-news/2017/jan/24/keystone-xl-dakota-access-pipelines-revived-trump-administration

110   https://edition.cnn.com/2020/07/06/politics/keystone-xl-supreme-court-pipeline/index.html

Greenhouse Gas

President Obama "presided over rising oil production" for the first seven years of his eight-year presidency, *Forbes* reported.[111] From a low point of 5.0 million barrels per day (bpd) in 2008, at the end of Bush's presidency, U.S. oil production grew each year to reach 9.4 million bpd in 2015—a gain of 88 percent during Obama's presidency until that point. In 2015, U.S. oil production reached a forty-four-year high. In 2016, *Forbes* noted, "This is in fact the largest domestic oil production increase during any presidency in U.S. history."

Similarly, the *Financial Times* observed that although Joe Biden promised during his 2020 presidential campaign to put climate change at the heart of an overhaul of the American energy system, "he served in an Obama administration that oversaw a historic surge in American oil and gas production, as shale went mainstream. Tens of thousands of wells were drilled and energy-bearing rocks fractured from North Dakota to Texas. And the industry cheered when the government he was part of lifted a ban on crude exports in 2015."[112]

The numbers over the long haul appear to reflect the Obama White House's approach to energy policy. In December 2008, the NOAA mean monthly reading for atmospheric carbon dioxide as measured at Mauna Loa (Hawaii) Observatory was 385.56 parts per million (ppm).[113] In December 2016 it was 404.42 ppm. Global temperatures rose as well during the same period, according to NASA's Goddard Institute for Space Studies. NASA/GISS measures the change in global surface temperatures relative to 1951–1980 average temperatures. In 2008 the reading was +.52C, while in 2016 it was +.99C.[114]

---

111   https://www.forbes.com/sites/rrapier/2016/01/15/president-obamas-petroleum-legacy/#1fd0be53c10f

112   https://www.ft.com/content/2ac477e7-34a4-4c0e-b9f4-018cef47d67d

113   https://www.co2.earth/monthly-co2

114   https://climate.nasa.gov/vital-signs/global-temperature/

PART III

FINANCE & ECONOMY

Bankers

Fraud was rife in the finance industry in the years preceding the 2008 stock market crash. Mortgage-backed securities were arbitrarily priced in favor of banking house sellers by the sellers themselves, and unrealistically high appraisals of the value of homes backing many of these mortgages were a common occurrence. Scams of all sorts involved thousands of people, including many with top positions in finance. But in the end only one high-level banker, Kareem Serageldin of Credit Suisse, was sent to prison.[115] He received two and a half years for arbitrarily hiking up prices for the bonds he managed.

Fifty firms paid out significant fines to governmental authorities. They also settled out of court with private parties. One major firm, Lehman Brothers, had to be liquidated.[116] Others were taken over by bigger institutions, fortified as they were by capital infusions from government bailout funds. The total bill for large Wall Street firms in terms of fines and settlements exceeded $150 billion.[117] Prison, however, was not in the cards for anyone working at these banks— Serageldin excepted.

Justice Department officials defended their reticent stance with regard to prosecution, claiming that it was too labor intensive and too resource consuming to pin badges of misconduct on specific individuals. But, as William D. Cohan noted in the *Atlantic*, "in light of various whistle-blower allegations—and the size of the settlements agreed to by the banks themselves—this explanation strains credulity."[118]

115   https://www.nytimes.com/2014/05/04/magazine/only-one-top-banker-jail-financial-crisis.html
116   https://money.cnn.com/2013/09/16/investing/lehman-brothers/index.html
117   https://www.cnbc.com/2015/04/30/7-years-on-from-crisis-150-billion-in-bank-fines-and-penalties.html
118   https://www.theatlantic.com/magazine/archive/2015/09/how-wall-streets-bankers-stayed-out-of-jail/399368/

The Justice Department did pursue one major case in late 2009 against two hedge fund operators at a major Wall Street bank.[119] They were found not guilty in a jury trial. Following the verdict, there was no criminal trial in federal court relating to the financial crash for another three years.

By late 2012, the five-year statute of limitations for criminal fraud from 2007 and earlier had run its course. However, there was still time to pursue alleged civil fraud by individuals. Federal officials' mode of operation, unfortunately, was not to focus on a specific, identifiable act of civil infraction at a firm and to seek damages for it. Rather, it was typically to review huge troves of documents and interview scores of employees about overall misconduct in order to determine how much of a settlement to extract from a given financial firm.

No one was punished individually, and no wonder. During a 2016 presidential debate with Bernie Sanders, Obama's former secretary of state Hillary Clinton remarked on the support her former boss enjoyed from the world of finance. "President Obama took more money from Wall Street in the 2008 campaign than anybody ever had," she said.[120] PolitiFact concurred that Obama broke the record in 2008 for Wall Street contributions, receiving $44.3 million from the finance, insurance, and real estate (FIRE) sector—or, to take a narrower measure more in keeping with what is traditionally thought of as Wall Street, $17.3 million from the securities and investment sector.[121]

As President Obama angrily reminded a group of bankers at a 2009 meeting, "My administration is the only thing between you and the pitchforks."[122] Angry he may have been, but compliant he certainly proved to be, especially in alleviating bankers' greatest fears.

---

119   https://www.nytimes.com/2009/11/11/business/11bear.html
120   https://www.nytimes.com/2016/03/07/us/politics/transcript-democratic-presidential-debate.html
121   https://www.politifact.com/factchecks/2016/mar/07/hillary-clinton/hillary-clinton-barack-obama-set-new-wall-street-f/
122   https://www.politico.com/story/2009/04/inside-obamas-bank-ceos-meeting-020871

Rubin

The Financial Crisis Inquiry Commission was set up by the Obama administration in May 2009 to ascertain who caused the 2007–2008 financial crash that led to the Great Recession. In late 2010, the commission voted to refer former Citigroup director Robert Rubin to the Department of Justice for investigation, stating that he "may have violated the laws of the United States in relation to the financial crisis."[123]

Rubin had served as U.S. Treasury secretary under Bill Clinton and pushed for the successful adoption of the Gramm–Leach–Bliley Act in 1999, which replaced the Glass–Steagall Act and removed the wall between commercial banks and investment banks. Joe Biden, an active proponent of the bill, was one of ninety senators who voted in its favor.[124] Rubin went on to make an estimated $126 million during his time at Citigroup from 1999 to 2009.

The commission alleged that Rubin, as chairman of the executive committee of Citi's board, may have been "culpable" in 2007 for misleading the bank's investors and the market in understating the extent of the bank's subprime loan exposure by 76 percent. The Obama administration ignored the commission's referral and no government action was ever brought against Rubin.

In retrospect, this is hardly surprising given that Citigroup, one of the largest donors to Obama's campaign, appears to have hand-selected his cabinet a month before the election that led to his presidency.[125] On October 6, 2008, as the financial crisis continued in full force, a Citigroup executive submitted to the Obama campaign a list of thirty-one names of preferred candidates for cabinet positions, according

---

123   https://fortune.com/2016/03/13/robert-rubin-financial-crisis-commission-justice-department/

124   https://archive.attn.com/stories/13313/joe-biden-reveals-the-congressional-vote-he-regrets-most

125   https://newrepublic.com/article/137798/important-wikileaks-revelation-isnt-hillary-clinton

to a 2016 WikiLeaks dump.[126] The list matched almost exactly the eventual makeup of Obama's cabinet. Included were three possibilities for Treasury secretary: Rubin himself, Larry Summers, and Timothy Geithner. Geithner, then-president of the Federal Reserve and a close cohort of Rubin's, was selected.

Only three days before the memo was sent, then-president George W. Bush had signed into law the Troubled Asset Relief Program (TARP), which handed over billions in taxpayer money to rescue the big banks. Citigroup was the biggest beneficiary, receiving $45 billion in cash in the form of a government stock purchase, as well as a $306 billion guarantee to shoulder losses on its flimsy mortgage-related assets.[127]

Just over a year into the Obama presidency, Rubin's "discreet" presence was being felt, asserted *Politico* in 2010.[128] "Behind the scenes, Rubin still wields enormous influence in Barack Obama's Washington, chatting regularly with a legion of former employees who dominate the ranks of the young administration's policy team. He speaks regularly to Treasury Secretary Timothy Geithner, who once worked for Rubin at Treasury."

126   https://wikileaks.org/podesta-emails/emailid/8190
127   https://www.wsws.org/en/articles/2016/10/15/wiki-o15.html
128   https://www.politico.com/story/2010/04/robert-rubin-returns-035515

AIG

In September 2008, shortly before insurance giant American International Group (AIG) was bailed out by the American taxpayer to the tune of $182 billion, Democratic vice president nominee Joe Biden expressed his opposition to the idea. "I don't think they should be bailed out by the federal government," he said On NBC's *Today Show*.[129] A day later, however, Biden changed his position, saying he needed more details. The shift followed a statement by presidential candidate Barack Obama declaring that any arrangement should protect families that counted on the company's insurance, but not its shareholders or management. "The truth is I don't know what the bailout is yet," Biden said in Mansfield, Ohio; "It looks like they're lending them a little bit of money."

Only months after receiving the bailout, AIG announced in March 2009 that it was awarding certain executives in its financial products division $165 million in bonuses.[130] It struck a nerve. An outraged New York Attorney General Andrew Cuomo divulged that seventy-three of these AIG employees were paid more than $1 million each under the plan: "AIG made more than 73 millionaires in the unit which lost so much money that it brought the firm to its knees, forcing a taxpayer bailout. Something is deeply wrong with this outcome."[131]

The announcement, coupled with news that total bonus outlays for AIG key personnel could reach $1.2 billion for the company as a whole, prompted widespread protests. Furious members of the public demonstrated in the streets near AIG's Connecticut headquarters, prompting a heavier-than-usual police presence, and AIG top executives received death threats.[132]

---

129   https://www.politico.com/story/2008/09/campaigns-struggle-to-craft-bailout-response-013552

130   https://www.nytimes.com/2009/03/15/business/15AIG.html

131   https://latimesblogs.latimes.com/money_co/2009/03/aig-bonuses-cuo.html

132   https://uk.reuters.com/article/us-financial-aig-threats-sb/aig-chief-worried-about-safety-after-death-threats-idUSTRE52H6ME20090318

President Obama spoke out against the bonuses in a statement on March 16, 2009:

"I want to comment on the news about executive bonuses at A.I.G. This is a corporation that finds itself in financial distress due to recklessness and greed. Under these circumstances, it's hard to understand how derivative traders at A.I.G. warranted any bonuses, much less $165 million in extra pay. How do they justify this outrage to the taxpayers who are keeping the company afloat? In the last six months, A.I.G. has received substantial sums from the U.S. Treasury. I've asked Secretary Geithner to use that leverage and pursue every legal avenue to block these bonuses and make the American taxpayers whole [. . .] This isn't just a matter of dollars and cents. It's about our fundamental values. All across the country, there are people who work hard and meet their responsibilities every day, without the benefit of government bailouts or multi-million dollar bonuses. And all they ask is that everyone, from Main Street to Wall Street to Washington, play by the same rules. That is an ethic we must demand. What this situation also underscores is the need for overall financial regulatory reform, so we don't find ourselves in this position again, and for some form of resolution mechanism in dealing with troubled financial institutions, so we have greater authority to protect the American taxpayer and our financial system in cases such as this. We will work with Congress to that end."[133]

Obama talked the progressive talk. He promised to try to use the leverage of the total $182 billion in loans that by then had been handed out by the Treasury Department and Federal Reserve as a means to block the $165 million in extra pay for AIG executives. The $165 million figure was less than one-tenth of 1 percent of the $182 billion lent by the federal government to AIG. But Obama did not succeed, even with leverage of over 1,000-to-1 in his favor.

---

133   https://thecaucus.blogs.nytimes.com/2009/03/16/obamas-statement-on-aig/

In the end, the House passed a resolution calling for a 90 percent tax on the bonuses, but the Senate never got around to considering it, despite widespread caterwauling by the public and politicians.[134] The bonus program was never stopped.

134   https://www.cbsnews.com/news/is-that-90-tax-on-aig-bonuses-dead/

Bankruptcy Law

For many years, Senator Joe Biden was a leading champion of measures to make it more difficult for individuals to file for bankruptcy and climb out of debt, finally resulting in the successful passage of the 2005 Bankruptcy Abuse Prevention and Consumer Protection Act (BAPCPA). The bill, beloved by credit card companies, increased the amount of money that needs to be repaid under Chapter 13, as well as the amount of paperwork and fees required to file for that form of bankruptcy. BAPCPA also made attorneys personally liable for inaccuracies in filings and added compliance obligations to small businesses. It created a means test that made it much harder for families with incomes over their state's median to file for Chapter 7 bankruptcy, and made all federal and private student loans nondischargeable.

Most Democratic senators, including Barack Obama, voted against the bill. Biden, however, was one of its first Democratic supporters, voting four times in its favor until it finally passed, reported the *New York Times*.[135] He also voted to prevent inclusion in the Act of protections for consumers and the vulnerable. According to the *Times*, Biden was

> "one of five Democrats in March 2005 who voted against a proposal to require credit card companies to provide more effective warnings to consumers about the consequences of paying only the minimum amount due each month. Mr. Obama voted for it. Mr. Biden also went against Mr. Obama to help defeat amendments aimed at strengthening protections for people forced into bankruptcy who have large medical debts or are in the military."

Prior to 2008, employees of MBNA, a powerful financial services company from Delaware, were major—and at one point the largest—contributors to Biden's campaigns.[136] Biden's son Hunter also worked

---

135   https://www.nytimes.com/2008/08/25/us/politics/25biden.html
136   https://www.propublica.org/article/bidens-cozy-relations-with-bank-industry-825

as an executive for MBNA upon his graduation from law school in 1996. After he left his job in 2001, he continued to receive consulting payments from MBNA. The company was bought in 2006 by Bank of America.

Campaigning for the presidency, Obama continued to display an apparent fervor for helping homeowners by enacting bankruptcy law reform. Specifically, he vowed to change the system wherein bankruptcy judges were barred from lowering mortgage payments on primary residences, although they could do so with vacation homes and other types of debt.[137] But Obama ultimately failed to live up to his pledge.

Instead, in 2009 he implemented the Home Affordable Modification Program (HAMP), which did not mandate banks to modify mortgages but only offered them incentives to do so. Obama promised it would assist 3 to 4 million homeowners to modify their loans to avoid foreclosure. But, "almost seven years into HAMP," reported the *Intercept*, "less than 1 million had received ongoing assistance; nearly one in three re-defaulted after receiving inadequate modifications; and 6 million families lost their homes over the same time period."[138]

In a 2013 civil lawsuit, six former Bank of America employees and one consultant blew the whistle on HAMP, describing it as a tool by the bank to string along struggling homeowners, squeezing them dry before eventually denying them permanent loan modifications.[139] They testified that they were instructed to lie to homeowners and to toss away documents or deliberately misplace them.

HAMP was terminated at the end of 2016. "Few noted its passage, but progressives should be happy to see it go" opined the *Intercept*.

137   https://www.propublica.org/article/dems-obama-broke-pledge-to-force-banks-to-help-homeowners

138   https://theintercept.com/2015/12/28/obama-program-hurt-homeowners-and-helped-big-banks-now-its-dead/

139   https://www.salon.com/2013/06/18/bank_of_america_whistleblowers_bombshell_we_were_told_to_lie/

"Perhaps no program of the Obama era did more significant—and possibly irreparable—damage to the promise of an activist government that can help solve the country's problems."

Solyndra and Other Grants to Cronies

In May 2010, Obama paid a visit to Solyndra, Inc., a Fremont, California solar panel manufacturer that was building a new facility with funding from the Recovery Act. A White House statement on the visit touted the new facility's creation of over three thousand construction-related jobs, and predicted the new factory could create up to one thousand long-term jobs.[140] Solyndra was the poster child for the Obama administration's purported attempt to create new jobs in the emerging field of clean energy by injecting it with billions of dollars in taxpayer-backed stimulus funds. "The true engine of economic growth will always be companies like Solyndra, will always be America's businesses," Obama said at the facility.

Two months prior to Obama's visit, Solyndra's auditor, PricewaterhouseCoopers, issued a warning that the company's financial problems "raise substantial doubt about its ability to continue as a going concern."[141] Six months afterward, Solyndra announced the layoffs of about 180 employees. In September 2011, less than a year since Obama's visit, Solyndra shut its doors, fired 1,100 workers, and announced it was filing for bankruptcy, leaving taxpayers bearing the cost of $535 million in loan guarantees.

In the wake of the Solyndra flameout, the Obama administration's green-energy loan program was the subject of a House probe into whether the president's political supporters were involved in influencing which companies received the taxpayer-backed funds through the Department of Energy's federally backed Section 1705 loan guarantee program.

140 https://obamawhitehouse.archives.gov/blog/2010/05/26/we-ve-got-go-back-making-things
141 https://www.aei.org/articles/export-import-banks-solyndra-subsidy-reeks-of-politicized-financing/

Nearly 90 percent of the loans guaranteed by the federal government from 2009 to 2011 went to subsidize lower-risk power plants, which in many cases were backed by big companies with vast resources, according to Veronique De Rugy, senior research fellow at Mercatus Center at George Mason University, who testified before members of the House.[142] As just one example, Cogentrix, a wholly owned subsidiary of the Goldman Sachs Group, Inc., received a $90 million guarantee through the program.

"Companies such as NRG Energy Inc.—closely linked to Senate Majority Leader Harry Reid—not only received $3.8 billion 1705 loans (almost a quarter of the total), but three subentities of the same company received a total of at least 39 grants under the stimulus law," wrote *U.S. News & World Report*.[143] "Like kids at Dairy Queen, these politically-connected companies filled their cones with soft-serve from the Department of Energy's Section 1705 loan guarantee program and then dipped it into the vast vat of taxpayer funding made available through President Barack Obama's economic stimulus program (the America Recovery and Reinvestment Act or ARRA)."

An ABC News and iWatch News investigation revealed that several of Obama's top campaign supporters went from soliciting political contributions to working from within the Energy Department as it disbursed the stimulus money.[144] One was Steven J. Spinner, a high-tech consultant and energy investor who raised at least $500,000 for Obama and went on to become one of Energy Secretary Steven Chu's key loan program advisors.[145] At the same time, Spinner's wife's law

---

142   https://www.mercatus.org/publications/government-spending/assessing-department-energy-loan-guarantee-program
143   https://www.usnews.com/opinion/blogs/nancy-pfotenhauer/2012/07/23/solyndra-cronyism-and-double-dipping-on-the-taxpayers-dime-
144   https://abcnews.go.com/Blotter/obama-fundraisers-ties-green-firms-federal-cash/story?id=14592626
145   https://abcnews.go.com/Blotter/obama-fundraiser-pushed-solyndra-deal-inside/story?id=14691618

firm represented several companies that applied for loans and received $2.4 million in federal funds for legal fees related to the Solyndra loan guarantee. Allison Spinner pledged to take no portion of the money and did not work on the loan applications.

Representatives for Steven and Allison Spinner and the Energy Department told ABC News and iWatch News that the couple had taken elaborate steps to avoid conflicts between his government work and her legal work. However, reported ABC News and iWatch News:

"Spinner described his job differently. He wrote in an online bio for the Center for American Progress, the left-leaning think tank he joined after leaving the administration, that he 'helped oversee the more than $100 billion of loan guarantee and direct lending authority' for the department's green-energy loan program. And in a speech at a 'Green Tech' conference in June 2010, Spinner described how he 'worked very, very closely with all the various organizations, the various offices, in trying to streamline operations and ... move the funding opportunity announcements out, get the solicitations out on the street.' 'What the Secretary really cared about was he wanted us to get the money out fast, he wanted us to pick and select fantastic projects,' Spinner said."[146]

---

146   https://abcnews.go.com/Blotter/obama-fundraisers-ties-green-firms-federal-cash/story?id=14592626

Geithner

The financial firm Morningstar Credit Ratings was found by the U.S. Securities and Exchange Commission (SEC) to have engaged in sales and marketing to prospective clients from mid-2015 to September 2016, violating a conflict of interest rule designed to separate business development from analytical activities.[147] The firm reached a settlement with the SEC in early 2020, agreeing to pay a sum of $3.5 million.

The Morningstar affair echoed a notorious pattern of behavior on the part of others in the industry in the previous decade. During the housing bubble that peaked in early 2006, rating agencies gave high ratings to mortgage-backed securities or bonds comprised of subprime mortgages and promoted these securities in order to get more ratings business from bond issuers.

An amendment to the Dodd–Frank bill proposed by Senator Al Franken in 2010 would have placed a firewall between bond issuers and rating issuers by forcing issuers to allow the SEC to choose the rating agencies that would rate their notes.[148] The incentive to give better-than-deserved ratings in order to get more business would have been destroyed. The amendment passed the Senate with sixty-five votes, but Obama's Treasury Secretary Timothy Geithner arranged, by his own admission, to have it killed in conference committee.[149] This conflict of interest remains extant.

147 https://www.reuters.com/article/us-usa-sec-morningstar-idUSKBN22R20Z
148 https://www.theatlantic.com/business/archive/2010/06/rating-agencies-escape-
financial-reform/58261/
149 https://cepr.net/there-was-a-solution-to-the-corruption-of-bond-rating-agencies-
timothy-geithner-killed-it/

Foreclosuregate

During the housing bubble, banks often failed to gather all necessary documents in making a mortgage, and after the bust, they often back-dated documents in order to make mortgages adequate. Many of these improperly created mortgages were foreclosed upon during the Great Recession, and in order for these foreclosures to take place, missing documents had to be created out of thin air, with bank employees signing hundreds of fraudulently backdated foreclosure-related documents a day without verifying or even reading them.[150] An *American Banker* investigation showed that as late as August 2011, "some of the largest mortgage servicers are still fabricating documents that should have been signed years ago and submitting them as evidence to foreclose on homeowners."[151]

In 2011, the federal government proposed a settlement of $20 billion from banks involved in these misdeeds.[152] Obama was pulled in opposite directions on this amount, which many observers found to be inadequate. He had previously told the public that his foreclosure-prevention methods would help up to 9 million homeowners. Ultimately, they only helped a small fraction of that number.

But Obama seemed hesitant about beefing up anti-foreclosure provisions. As *Slate* put it: "since the midterm elections Obama has been trying to position his administration as pro-business. Forcing a hefty settlement on the banks would not be seen as pro-business."[153]

Widespread resentment festered toward banks that had expedited foreclosures with fake documents. George Goehl, co-executive

---

150   https://slate.com/business/2011/03/foreclosuregate-settlement-is-20-billion-too-much-or-too-little.html

151   https://www.americanbanker.com/news/robo-signing-redux-servicers-still-fabricating-foreclosure-documents

152   https://www.wsj.com/articles/SB10001424052748703842004576162813248586844

153   https://slate.com/business/2011/03/foreclosuregate-settlement-is-20-billion-too-much-or-too-little.html

director of National People's Action, which coordinated with thousands of homeowners, maintained that the $20-billion proposed settlement was virtually nil, and that nothing short of criminal prosecution of senior level bankers would be acceptable.[154]

Not one criminal prosecution of these senior level bankers took place.

---

154   https://www.huffingtonpost.co.uk/entry/foreclosure-fraud-prosecutions_n_828333

HSBC

A 2012 report on HSBC issued by the U.S. Senate Permanent Subcommittee on Investigations found that the bank had failed to stop money laundering, totaling at least $881 million, by clients who happened to be known members of Mexican drug cartels.[155] HSBC was also found to have obfuscated hundreds of billions of dollars' worth of transfers for clients in Iran, Sudan, Libya, Burma, and Cuba, in clear violation of federal economic sanctions imposed against those countries.

A few months later, the Justice Department decided against criminally indicting the bank, and instead reached a settlement with no individual going to jail.[156] The settlement instead directed HSBC to pay a fine of $1.92 billion. An editorial in the *New York Times* blasted the settlement as "a dark day for the rule of law" because it showed that some banks were "too big to indict."[157]

The bank was specifically accused of allowing non-monitored wire transfers of more than $670 *billion* and giving its okay on more than $9.4 billion in purchases of U.S. cash from HSBC Mexico, clearly money-laundering operations. Any individual found guilty of violating the requirement to report to the government more than $10,000 in cash transactions in one day faces up to five years in federal prison. This includes agents of entities responsible for failure to report as well. Under the HSBC settlement, no individual was penalized in any way.

Justice Department officials claimed that entering criminal charges based on an indictment against HSBC for money laundering would essentially destroy the bank, because it would by law be cut off from some major clients, such as pension funds. The DOJ argued,

155 https://www.hsgac.senate.gov/imo/media/doc/PSI%20REPORT-HSBC%20CASE%20
HISTORY%20(9.6).pdf

156 https://dealbook.nytimes.com/2012/12/10/hsbc-said-to-near-1-9-billion-settlement-
over-money-laundering/

157 http://www.nytimes.com/2012/12/12/opinion/hsbc-too-big-to-indict.html

somewhat unconvincingly, that "HSBC would almost surely have lost its banking license in the U.S., the future of the institutions would have been under threat and the entire banking system would have been destabilized."[158]

This creates a "moral hazard" because the bank, if acting rationally, would continue its malfeasance, since it is too big to fail and would be left alone, regardless of whatever misdeeds it stood accused of engaging in. The threat of criminal enforcement as a deterrent to the commission of a felony has fallen by the wayside.

"We accept responsibility for our past mistakes [and] we are committed to protecting the integrity of the global financial system," said HSBC's chief executive, Stuart T. Gulliver, in a dubiously contrite statement.[159] In the course of investigating the bank, federal investigators also detected another "past mistake": the movement of laundered money by HSBC to Saudi banks such as al-Qaeda ally Al Rajhi, as well as other Saudi financial institutions with ties to terrorist groups. No repercussions there, either.

158   https://observer.com/2014/11/obama-pick-for-ag-let-hsbc-off-the-hook/
159   https://www.itv.com/news/update/2012-12-11/hsbc-chief-we-accept-responsibility-for-our-past-mistakes/

Campaign Finance

In late 2015, a group of progressives took President Obama to task for his failure to live up to promises on campaign finance reform. The nonprofit activist organization Rootstrikers released a report with an accompanying statement that accused him of doing nothing to rectify wrongs and of making things worse in several key areas.[160] The report faulted him on a number of points, including failing to act and being proactively involved in dismantling existing campaign finance regulations. A spokesman for Rootstrikers, which was formed to fight political corruption and special interest money in elections, predicted a legacy of failure for Obama on the issue of campaign finance.

The report's major points were:

- Although prodded by good government organizations, the president did not utilize an executive order function that was fully within his power—namely, to order federal contractors to declare their campaign contributions.
- He signed into law a bill passed by Congress that allowed for the raising of limits on campaign contributions by big donors. He also signed legislation to abolish public financing of party conventions. Much of this legislation was included in the 2014 "Cromnibus" spending bill.
- He ignored press questions about dark money.
- The Obama-appointed chairwoman of the Securities and Exchange Commission, Mary Jo White, killed a proposal that would have required publicly traded companies to disclose their campaign contributions.
- Tom Wheeler, the chairman of the Federal Election Commission, who was also appointed by Obama, stated that

---

160   https://www.motherjones.com/politics/2015/12/campaign-finance-activists-assail-obamas-record/

requiring further disclosure of sponsors of campaign ads was "not a priority."

- Obama's IRS director postponed the implementation of rules that would have clarified what nonprofits were allowed to do in elections.

- On his campaign trail, Obama left a trail of broken promises. He failed to become a vocal booster for public financing and allowed fundraising for super-PACs by friends and associates, as well as corporate contributions to go toward paying off his second inaugural expenses.

- He disregarded pleas from campaign finance reform activists to appoint FEC commissioners who would work across the aisle, rather than along party lines.

Revolving Door

Campaigning for the presidency in 2008, Obama put voters on notice: "I am in this race to tell the corporate lobbyists that their days of setting the agenda in Washington are over."[161] His first executive order after assuming office, the White House said, "closes the revolving door that allows government officials to move to and from private sector jobs in ways that give that sector undue influence over government."[162]

But toward the end of his second term, Obama faced mounting criticism for the speed and degree with which his revolving door had been spinning.

Declaring his promise "a lie," the *Washington Examiner* noted in January 2016 that from the start of the Obama presidency, "dozens of lobbyists were in policymaking jobs, including a Raytheon lobbyist as deputy secretary of Defense, a Goldman Sachs lobbyist as Treasury chief of staff, a lobbyist for the Swiss Bankers' Association as general counsel at the IRS and four lobbyists in his cabinet."[163]

The *Guardian* struck much the same tone: "a rash of senior White House staff jumping ship for well-paid lobbying jobs at some of America's biggest and most controversial companies could pose a threat to open government, governance and transparency campaigners have warned."[164]

An investigation by the *Intercept* found that Google representatives alone had attended White House meetings more than once a week, on average, from the time Obama entered the White House

---

161 https://www.theguardian.com/us-news/2015/mar/07/washington-revolving-door-lobbying-jobs-obama

162 https://obamawhitehouse.archives.gov/21stcenturygov/actions/revolving-door

163 https://www.washingtonexaminer.com/eight-years-later-obamas-broken-promise-on-the-revolving-door

164 https://www.theguardian.com/us-news/2015/mar/07/washington-revolving-door-lobbying-jobs-obama

through October 2015.[165] "Nearly 250 people have shuttled from government service to Google employment or vice versa over the course of his administration," according to the report.

Here is a short list of White House staff and administration officials who sauntered through the revolving door on Obama's watch:

- Jay Carney, White House press secretary, left to become head of global corporate affairs at Amazon.
- David Plouffe, Obama campaign manager and senior White House adviser, left to become senior vice president of policy and strategy at Uber.
- Alyssa Mastromonaco, White House deputy chief of staff for operations, left to become chief operating officer at Vice Media.
- Samuel Maruca, director of transfer pricing (multinational company taxation) at the Internal Revenue Service, joined law firm Covington Burling as partner, to lead on helping multinationals create "tax-efficient structuring."
- Budget chief Peter Orzsag, left for Citibank.
- General counsel Greg Craig, left for Goldman Sachs.
- Deputy chief of staff, Mona Sutphen, left for Swiss bank UBS.
- Energy efficiency czar Cathy Zoi, left to join a George Soros-run investment firm specializing in green energy.
- David Stevens, who ran the Federal Housing Authority (which subsidizes mortgage lenders), left for the Mortgage Bankers Association.
- Humana lobbyist Liz Fowler, who crafted the Obamacare law for the Department of Health and Human Services, left to become a top lobbyist at Johnson and Johnson.

- Marilyn Tavenner, who implemented many of Obamacare's subsidies and rules for insurers, left the Centers for Medicare & Medicaid Services to become the top lobbyist at the insurers' biggest group, America's Health Insurance Plans. She was replaced by Andy Slavitt, former executive at United Health.
- Intellectual property enforcement czar Victoria Espinel, who worked with the Commerce Department overseeing efforts to enforce copyright, trademark, and patent protections, left to become president and CEO of the Business Software Alliance.
- Tom Power, who as deputy chief technology officer at the White House was involved in numerous discussions about new broadband net neutrality rules, left to become the top lawyer for the mobile-phone industry's trade group, CTIA The Wireless Association.
- Scientist Daniel Fabricant, acting CEO and vice president of global government and scientific affairs for the dietary supplement industry trade group, the Natural Products Association, left to become director of the Division of Dietary Supplement Programs at the Food and Drug Administration. He later returned to the trade group as its CEO and executive director.
- Robert Khuzami joined the Securities and Exchange Commission as head of its enforcement division. His previous employer, Deutsche Bank AG, was at the center of the global financial collapse.
- Rahm Emanuel, former partner at a Chicago investment bank, became White House chief of staff.
- Larry Summers, former managing director of a hedge fund, became Obama's chief economic adviser.
- Herbert Allison, a Merrill Lynch executive, became assistant secretary of the treasury, overseeing TARP.
- Lewis Alexander, former chief economist at Citigroup, became counselor to the Treasury secretary.

- Adam Storch, former vice president of Goldman Sachs' Business Intelligence Group, became managing executive of the SEC's Division of Enforcement
- Gary Gensler, a partner at Goldman Sachs, became chairman of the Commodity Futures Trading Commission
- Karthik Ramanathan, a foreign exchange dealer at Goldman Sachs, became acting assistant treasury secretary for financial markets.

SEC Chairmen

During his time as president, Obama sequentially appointed two chairmen of the Securities Exchange Commission (SEC), the federal agency that is tasked with regulating securities markets and protecting investors. The first appointee was Mary Schapiro, who served from 2009 to 2012. Schapiro was succeeded by Mary Jo White, who held the position until January 2017. (Elisse Walter also served for a short interregnum of about four months.)

Schapiro, in an exquisite example of the public-to-private-sector phenomenon, left her post to join Promontory Financial Group, a firm founded by a former head of the Office of the Comptroller of the Currency.[166] As for her role in regulating the stock markets, she received "faint praise" as the *Economist* put it, adding that: "If the goal of the SEC is to serve as the investor's advocate, there is not much for Ms. Schapiro to crow about."[167]

Enforcement actions did increase under Schapiro's leadership, but the SEC was tasked by Congress, in accord with Dodd–Frank regulations, to write seventy-six rules by the approximate date Schapiro left office. Nevertheless, the agency missed the deadline on fifty of them. And for all its vaunted enforcement capability, no success was achieved in prosecuting any of the "big fish" who had made ill-gotten millions during the 2007–2008 crash. Only furtive attempts were made to bring these individuals to justice.

The appointment of Mary Jo White to head up the SEC following Schapiro (during Obama's second term) only bolstered the widespread opinion that the president had gone easy on Wall Street. As Matt Taibbi put it in a 2013 *Rolling Stone* article:

---

166 https://www.theguardian.com/business/2013/apr/02/mary-schapiro-sec-revolving-door

167 https://www.economist.com/finance-and-economics/2012/12/01/a-mixed-record

"I was shocked when I heard that Mary Jo White, a former U.S. Attorney and a partner for the white-shoe Wall Street defense firm Debevoise and Plimpton, had been named the new head of the SEC. I thought to myself: [...] couldn't they have found someone who isn't a perfect symbol of the revolving-door culture under which regulators go soft on suspected Wall Street criminals, knowing they have million-dollar jobs waiting for them at hotshot defense firms as long as they play nice with the banks while still in office?"[168]

By 2016, the progressive wing of the Democratic Party membership in Congress was aghast. Senator Elizabeth Warren sent a letter to Obama urging him to fire White, regardless of the fact that it was mere weeks prior to the presidential election.[169] What got Warren's goat, among other things, was White's unwillingness to move forward on political spending disclosure reform. This would have forced corporations to disclose their political contributions, introducing an entirely new level of transparency by publicly traded firms.

"Chair White's refusal to move forward on a political spending disclosure rule serves the narrow interests of powerful executives who would prefer to hide their expenditures of company money to advance their own personal ideologies," Warren wrote.

White, like her predecessor at the SEC, Schapiro, simply refused to take this glaring need seriously. Political disclosure proposals languish to this day. One recent bill, introduced in the U.S. House of Representatives in February 2019, would have required publicly traded corporations to disclose all expenditures made for political activities.[170] It never made it out of the House Committee on Financial Services.

168   https://www.rollingstone.com/politics/politics-news/choice-of-mary-jo-white-to-head-sec-puts-fox-in-charge-of-hen-house-185463/
169   https://www.cnbc.com/2016/10/14/sen-elizabeth-warren-urges-president-obama-to-designate-new-sec-chair.html
170   https://stateandfed.com/lobbycomply/campaign-finance/the-corporate-political-disclosure-act-of-2019-introduced-in-u-s-congress/

National Debt

On January 20, 2009, the day Barack Obama was sworn in as president, the national debt stood at $10.626 trillion. By the time he left office eight years later, it equaled $19.947 trillion.[171] Obama raised the national debt by more than $9 trillion, or 87 percent, more than any other president. This represents a $28,000 burden for every man, woman, and child in the United States. Rich and poor alike each shoulder the same share of the national debt, which in mid-2016 stood at around $60,000 per capita, including the $28,000 that Obama added. This amount is close to the net worth of the typical American, but only 6 percent of a millionaire's net worth, making for a profoundly unfair situation.

It does not look like things will change any time soon. The national debt has soared to over $26 trillion under Trump, and one estimate puts the increase for 2020 alone at $4 trillion, the product of massive federal spending on coronavirus relief measures.[172] A *Forbes* report of September 2020 stated that presidential candidate Joe Biden's policy proposals would add close to $2 trillion to the national debt by 2030.[173]

171   https://www.thebalance.com/national-debt-under-obama-3306293
172   https://www.businessinsider.com/national-debt-total-trillion-record-federal-government-coronavirus-spending-2020-6
173   https://www.forbes.com/sites/shaharziv/2020/09/15/biden-policy-proposals-would-grow-debt-2-trillion-by-2030-reduce-it-61-percent-by-2050/

Economic Growth

Barack Obama emerged last among postwar presidents in terms of the economic growth achieved during his two terms in office, as measured by Gross Domestic Product. He is the only one to leave office having failed to achieve a single quarter of 3-percent growth.

From 1946 through the second quarter of 2016, average annual real GDP growth in the United States was 2.9 percent.[174] Obama averaged 1.5 percent. Here is the average annual real GDP growth by postwar president (in descending order):

Johnson (1964-68), 5.3%

Kennedy (1961-63), 4.3%

Clinton (1993-2000), 3.9%

Reagan (1981-88), 3.5%

Carter (1977-80), 3.3%

Eisenhower (1953-60), 3.0%

(Post-WWII average: 2.9%)

Nixon (1969-74), 2.8%

Ford (1975-76), 2.6%

G. H. W. Bush (1989-92), 2.3%

G. W. Bush (2001-08), 2.1%

Truman (1946-52), 1.7%

Obama (2009-15), 1.5%

Obama came in dead last.

From a progressive perspective, of course, economic growth is not necessarily a virtue. Economic growth that relies upon ecological degradation, for example, is not valuable in itself. And growth that only benefits a thin sliver at the top is anathema to the progressive agenda. But if growth is relatively egalitarian and environmentally clean, then it may be considered quality growth. Unfortunately, the small quantity of growth achieved under Obama was not made up for by its quality.

---

174   https://www.hudson.org/research/12714-economic-growth-by-president

Corporate Profits

At the end of Obama's presidency, corporate profits were up by 144 percent since he took office, while average weekly earnings for all workers were up by 4 percent.[175]

---

175   https://www.factcheck.org/2016/10/obamas-numbers-october-2016-update/

Forbes 400

The total wealth of the Forbes 400 reached $2.4 trillion in 2016. It was $1.57 trillion in 2008, and $1 trillion in 1998 (all figures are in real 2016 dollars).[176]

The richest person on the 2008 Forbes 400 list had a net worth of $57 billion, while the richest in 2016 was worth $81 billion (both years the person was Bill Gates).[177]

In 2016, a net worth of $1.7 billion was required to join the Forbes 400, whereas only $1.3 billion was required in 2008.

176 https://oregonstate.edu/instruct/anth484/forbes.html;https://www.forbes.com/sites/
kerryadolan/2016/10/04/inside-the-2016-forbes-400-facts-and-figures-about-
americas-richest-people/

177 https://www.forbes.com/2008/09/16/richest-american-billionaires-lists-400list08-
cx_mm_dg_0917richintro.html

Corporate Cash Abroad

At the end of 2011, U.S. corporations held a combined total of $1.6 trillion abroad, avoiding American taxes on profits earned overseas.[178] By 2017 that figure had grown to $2.6 trillion, an increase of $1 trillion in six years.[179]

178   https://www.bloomberg.com/news/articles/2012-03-02/cash-horde-expands-by-187-billion-in-untaxed-offshore-accounts

179   https://money.cnn.com/2017/11/03/news/companies/romans-numeral-overseas-cash/index.html

PART IV

FOREIGN POLICY

Drones

On January 23, 2009, as a new president, Barack Obama ordered his first two drone strikes. They targeted Pakistan and killed as many as twenty civilians. By the end of his first year in office, Obama had carried out more drone strikes than had George W. Bush during his entire two-term presidency. Two terms in, Obama had 542 strikes under his belt, ten times as many as Bush.[180] The Obama–Biden administration incorrectly maintained that drones were precise enough to pick off a terrorist without any collateral damage to bystanders. In total, the administration's strikes killed 3,797 people, 324 of whom were civilians.

The targets were plucked from the U.S. government's main terrorist database. In 2014, the U.S. acknowledged that 469,000 people had been nominated the previous year for inclusion in this repository of "known or suspected terrorists."[181] The basis for qualification could be as flimsy as a single uncorroborated Facebook or Twitter post. Of the nearly half a million nominees, a mere 4,900 were rejected. One of those retained in the database was Abdulrahman al-Aulaqi, a sixteen-year-old apolitical American citizen who was killed by a U.S. drone strike in Yemen in October 2011.

Although the drone program was vilified by the progressive wing of the Democratic Party, it was embraced not only by Obama but by his vice president. Joe Biden, to whom Obama devolved significant foreign policy influence, championed a combination of drone strikes and special forces to fight terrorism, an approach he called "counterterrorism plus."[182]

180 https://www.cfr.org/blog/obamas-final-drone-strike-data
181 https://www.washingtonpost.com/opinions/obamas-drone-war-is-a-shameful-part-of-his-legacy/2016/05/05/a727eea8-12ea-11e6-8967-7ac733c56f12_story.html
182 https://jacobinmag.com/2018/08/joe-biden-democratic-party-military-hawk

Independent peace activist Noam Chomsky called out the Obama administration in March 2015 for launching "the most extensive global terrorism campaign" the world had yet seen:

> "This is the drone assassination campaign, which officially is aimed at killing people who *the administration believes* might someday intend to harm the U.S., and killing anyone else who happens to be nearby. There has been really nothing like that in the past. This is quite an innovation in the history of international terrorism. It is also a terrorism generating campaign—that is well understood by people in high places. When you murder somebody in a Yemen village, and maybe a couple of other people who are standing there, the chances are pretty high that others will want to take revenge."[183]

This is commonly known as blowback.

183 https://www.realclearpolitics.com/video/2015/03/19/noam_chomsky_obamas_ drone_assassination_program_is_the_most_extensive_global_terrorism_campaign_ the_world_has_yet_seen.html

Arms

According to a report by the Stockholm International Peace Research Institute, more than $160 billion in foreign arms sales by the United States took place during President Obama's first five years in office.[184] Armament sales during this period outpaced by $30 billion those of George W. Bush's entire eight years as president. The unprecedented sales took place under the auspices of the Department of Defense's Foreign Military Sales (FMS) program.

In addition, during the period from 2010 to 2014, the U.S. was the world's largest international arms dealer, commanding 31 percent of all military weapons sales in the international arms market.[185]

By the end of his eight years in the White House, Barack Obama had approved more than $278 billion in foreign arms sales, more than double the amount from the previous eight years of Bush, according to the Defense Security Cooperation Agency, which is part of the Department of Defense.[186]

184 https://www.breitbart.com/border/2015/04/22/nobel-peace-prize-winner-obama-is-now-largest-international-arms-dealer-since-wwii/

185 https://www.sipri.org/sites/default/files/files/FS/SIPRIFS1503.pdf

186 https://www.defenseone.com/business/2016/11/obamas-final-arms-export-tally-more-doubles-bushs/133014/

Haiti

Haiti's manufacturing sector is dominated by non-Haitian contractors who produce merchandise for American companies such as Hanes, Levi's, and Fruit of the Loom. The minimum wage in the Haitian garment industry was an incredible 24 cents an hour well into the early years of this century. In June 2009, the Haitian Parliament unanimously passed a law to raise the minimum wage to 61 cents an hour, or five dollars a day, about one-fifth of the income needed to maintain a small household's minimal cost of living. Foreign textile industry representatives and factory owners were aghast at this presumptuous move and the Obama–Biden administration vigorously supported them.

Objections to raising the wage were specifically brought forth by the U.S. State Department and the U.S. Agency for International Development. David E. Lindwall, a deputy chief of mission for the U.S. Embassy, opposed the hike to five dollars a day as apparently too profligate, saying that it "did not take economic reality into account." [187]

In a 2011 article, the *Columbia Journalism Review* put things into perspective with the following exercise:

"Haiti has about 25,000 garment workers. If you paid each of them $2 a day more, it would cost their employers $50,000 per working day, or about $12.5 million a year. Zooming in on specific companies helps clarify this even more. As of last year [2010] Hanes had 3,200 Haitians making t-shirts for it. Paying each of them two bucks a day more would cost it about $1.6 million a year. Hanesbrands Incorporated made $211 million on $4.3 billion in sales last year, and presumably it would pass on at least some of its higher labor costs to consumers. Or better yet, Hanesbrands CEO Richard Noll could forgo some of his rich compensation package. He could pay for the raises for those

---

187   https://www.thenation.com/article/archive/wikileaks-haiti-let-them-live-3-day/

3,200 t-shirt makers with just one-sixth of the $10 million in salary and bonus he raked in last year."[188]

Nonetheless, the Obama administration and private interests succeeded in capping the garment workers' minimum wage at 31 cents an hour. And there it remained until 2014, when a new law established it at 64 cents an hour, still well below the $1.42 an hour demanded at the time by Haitian workers.[189]

On January 12, 2010, a disaster of unfathomable dimensions struck Haiti in the form of an earthquake that killed hundreds of thousands of people. Obama and the Pentagon organized a massive, well-funded aid effort. Some viewed this purported disaster relief effort as a disguised military occupation, considering that Secretary of State Hillary Clinton quickly declared full command of Haiti's airport and airspace on behalf of the U.S., which then restricted humanitarian missions from other countries.[190] At least 17,000 U.S. military personnel were sent to Haiti and U.S. Navy and Coast Guard ships surrounded the beleaguered island nation.[191]

In 2011, while recovery from the earthquake was still tentative, a local well-known singer and music business luminary, Michel Martelly, became the president of Haiti. He was sworn in following a hotly contested run-off election, endorsed by the Organization of American States and Secretary of State Hillary Clinton, the latter of whom had pushed for the withdrawal of incumbent president René

188 https://archives.cjr.org/the_audit/a_pulled_scoop_shows_us_booste.php
189 https://www.nytimes.com/2014/05/06/world/americas/haiti-minimum-wage-increases.html
190 https://www.theguardian.com/world/2010/jan/17/us-accused-aid-effort-haiti; https://www.telegraph.co.uk/news/worldnews/centralamericaandthecaribbean/haiti/7020093/Haiti-earthquake-France-criticises-US-occupation.html
191 https://edition.cnn.com/2010/WORLD/americas/01/26/haiti.by.the.numbers/index.html?hpt=T1

Préval's favored successor.[192] Despite Haitian opposition to holding national elections in the wake of the earthquake, the U.S., France, and Canada reportedly paid $29 million in logistical support to ensure that they happened. In the end, 71 percent of registered voters failed to turn out, no doubt reflecting the arbitrary exclusion of the largest political party, Fanmi Lavalas.[193] OAS "experts" intervened to throw out 234 tally sheets, changing the election results.[194] Wrote journalism professor and author Amy Wilentz in the *L.A. Times*, "According to many sources, including the president himself, the international community has threatened Preval with immediate exile if he does not bow to their interpretation of election results."[195]

Four years later, after expired terms had brought the number of elected officials in Haiti to under a dozen, Martelly began to rule by decree. He surrounded himself with associates who had been arrested for rape, murder, and large-scale drug running.[196] Many non-associates of the president stopped attending palace events, feeling uncomfortable around security guards who had been arrested for murder. Martelly organized a paramilitary unit to enforce his edicts, by threat of or by actual violence.

The U.S. Embassy, aside from making occasional appeals for calm, had nothing to say about the paramilitary force and refrained from condemning human rights violations by the national government. When Martelly's thugs were blamed for throwing rocks and bottles and ripping up voting materials at precincts to disrupt the election for

---

192   https://www.csmonitor.com/World/Americas/2011/0131/Hillary-Clinton-presses-Haiti-s-Rene-Preval-to-break-election-stalemate

193   https://web.archive.org/web/20200119164708/http://cepr.net/publications/reports/haitis-fatally-flawed-election

194   https://www.theguardian.com/commentisfree/cifamerica/2011/jan/18/haiti-usa

195   https://www.latimes.com/archives/la-xpm-2011-jan-16-la-oe-wilentz-haiti-20110116-story.html

196   https://www.nytimes.com/2015/03/17/world/americas/haitian-president-tightens-grip-as-scandal-engulfs-circle-of-friends.html

legislative seats in August 2015, the Embassy was largely taciturn.[197] According to the *Hill*, this was a "sham election" with only 18 percent of registered voters going to the polls, and 23 percent of all votes never being counted due to fraud and violence on election day.[198] After the October 2015 presidential election was annulled, following similar allegations of widespread fraud, a second election was held in 2016. Martelly's chosen successor, Jovenel Moïse, won the presidency.[199]

197 https://uk.reuters.com/article/us-haiti-election/haitis-first-election-in-four-years-marred-by-sporadic-violence-idUSKCN0QE09H20150809

198 https://thehill.com/blogs/congress-blog/foreign-policy/256679-haiti-us-interference-wins-elections

199 https://www.bbc.co.uk/news/world-latin-america-38900743

Honduras

The democratically elected government of President Manuel Zelaya in Honduras was overthrown in a military coup in June 2009. The coup produced an upsurge in right-wing violence against indigenous activists, environmentalists, liberals, and journalists. The new regime set up a presidential election, held that November, the results of which were viewed as deeply flawed by a wide range of political observers. Thus, the coup perpetrators and their allies effectively won.

According to a report by the Tegucigalpa-based COFADEH (Committee of Families of the Detained and Disappeared of Honduras), in the two months that followed the coup, more than 1,100 instances of arbitrary detentions, attacks on the media, outright killings, and other forms of human rights violations took place. Yet the U.S. refused to legally designate the overthrow of Zelaya a coup, which would have barred any sort of assistance to Honduras.[200]

Where did the U.S. president and his advisors stand on this? After making a few timid statements regarding the illegality of the coup and the importance of democracy, the Obama administration did "quite a bit to help the coup government succeed," wrote the *Guardian*.[201]

On March 9, 2012, ninety-four Democratic representatives, nearly half the House Democratic membership, requested that the Obama administration suspend assistance to Honduran military and police. They cited widespread allegations of serious human rights violations on the part of Honduran security forces as credible. Particular attention was given over to the Bajo Aguan region, where, according to the representatives, forty-five peasant-rights activists had been killed by

---

200 https://www.reuters.com/article/us-honduras-usa-sb/obama-says-coup-in-honduras-is-illegal-idUKTRE55S5J220090629
201 https://www.theguardian.com/commentisfree/cifamerica/2012/mar/22/democrats-press-obama-us-complicity-honduras

security forces and private agents working for landowners since the coup.

This request, and a nearly simultaneous letter by a group of senators who laid out similar concerns, were ignored in the mainstream American media. State Department spokesperson Victoria Nuland responded with a statement that did not square with the House members' request. "I think the concerns that we have with this particular proposal is that it calls for a cutting of all aid to Honduras ... this recommendation to cut it all off is a relatively blunt instrument," she said.[202] This was despite the fact that the lawmakers had not wanted to cut off all aid, only military and police assistance.

The Obama–Biden administration had already added fuel to the fire by increasing military aid to Honduras for fiscal year 2012. Mexico was the only other Latin American country deemed deserving of such a boost. Why? The reason given was the War on Drugs. Vowing to defeat drug traffickers and fight corruption, Vice President Joe Biden met with Central American leaders in Honduras in March 2012.[203] During the visit, he reiterated the administration's pledge to boost aid even further for upcoming fiscal year 2013—from $105 million to $107 million. "One of the areas in which we will hopefully be of help is in vetting the police, the prosecutors and the judges," Biden said.

202 https://www.theguardian.com/commentisfree/cifamerica/2012/mar/22/democrats-press-obama-us-complicity-honduras
203 https://edition.cnn.com/2012/03/06/world/americas/honduras-biden/index.html

Blackwater

Military contractor Blackwater was founded in 1997 by former Navy Seal Erik Prince. The private security firm, which later went by the names Xe and Academi, provided manpower to American agencies working and fighting throughout the world. Blackwater could best be described as a provider of mercenaries to American interests in global hotspots, as well as to foreign entities in need of trained American ex-military personnel. The company earned more than $1 billion protecting U.S. facilities and personnel during the Iraq war.[204] In 2007, Blackwater achieved an unwanted reputation after four of its employees killed seventeen Iraqi non-combatants in Baghdad. They were convicted of the deaths in 2014.[205]

This incident did not put a crimp on Blackwater's earnings ability. In 2010, under the auspices of the Obama administration, the CIA awarded Xe a $100 million service contract to "secure its bases" in Afghanistan, while the State Department awarded a separate contract worth $120 million.[206] Three years later, an Academi subsidiary and the Department of State signed a $92 million-dollar commitment to provide security services to American embassies throughout the world.[207]

Despite President Obama publicly expressing misgivings over the use of private contractors in potential armed engagements, the contracts were allowed to go through under his watch. Moreover, also under Obama, in July 2012, the U.S. Army awarded Academi a contract in the amount of nearly $6.7 million to "provide for the life support services in Afghanistan."[208] In May 2014, that contract received an additional $8.8 million modification, with the mission stating that

204 https://foreignpolicy.com/2014/07/01/blackwaters-descendants-are-doing-just-fine/
205 https://www.nytimes.com/2014/10/23/us/blackwater-verdict.html
206 https://www.theguardian.com/world/2010/jun/28/blackwater-wins-afghanistan-contract
207 https://foreignpolicy.com/2014/07/01/blackwaters-descendants-are-doing-just-fine/
208 https://content.govdelivery.com/accounts/USDOD/bulletins/4b5ef5

Academi was to provide "camp integrity and life support and private security services."[209] Between 2012 and 2014, yet another $16 million in modifications was added to this particular contract, for a total contract value of $31 million.

Stories and testimonies of witnesses to Blackwater's behavior are legion. In just once instance, a State Department investigator in Iraq was threatened with death by a top Blackwater manager in the country.[210] Two other clear examples of the controversies surrounding Blackwater were its alleged export of illegal weapons to Afghanistan and its attempt to secure lucrative defense contracts in South Sudan in clear violation of U.S. sanctions in the country.[211]

Prince, the Blackwater founder, had comfortable connections with top figures in the George W. Bush White House and the CIA, and was a major element in a four-year federal investigation into allegations of Blackwater's sanctions violations, bribery, and its flouting of the Foreign Corrupt Practices Act in Southern Sudan and Iraq.

The Obama administration, however, decided not to press criminal charges against Blackwater. Instead, it reached a $42 million settlement with the company in 2010 for its hundreds of violations of U.S. export control regulations.[212]

209 https://thinkprogress.org/after-threatening-to-murder-government-official-blackwater-awarded-over-200-million-in-contracts-c97526bb1425/
210 http://www.newsweek.com/blackwater-employee-threatened-kill-state-department-investigator-report-256797
211 https://www.mcclatchydc.com/news/nation-world/world/article24586396.html
212 https://www.nytimes.com/2010/08/21/world/21blackwater.html

Libya

Barack Obama told Fox News in 2016 that "failing to plan for the day after" the ousting of Libyan leader Muammar Gaddafi was the worst mistake of his presidency. Nonetheless, he said, he felt that intervening in Libya had been "the right thing to do."[213] Despite claiming to be "strongly against going to Libya" earlier in 2011, Vice President Joe Biden ultimately agreed with Obama, stating on the day of Gaddafi's death that "The people of Libya have gotten rid of a dictator [...] NATO got it right."[214]

Libya was described by various media outlets as chaotic and anarchic after Gaddafi was captured and killed by rebel fighters in October 2011. Rival militias and governments fought for dominance and the Islamic State of Iraq and Syria (ISIS) gained traction. In an interview with the *Atlantic* near the end of his presidency, Obama placed part of the blame for the failed intervention on British prime minister David Cameron and French president Nicolas Sarkozy.[215] Cameron, he said, had become distracted, and "Sarkozy wanted to trumpet the flights he was taking in the air campaign, despite the fact that we had wiped out all the air defenses and essentially set up the entire infrastructure." Obama said Libyan tribal divisions had also played a role, as they had been greater than predicted.

After being notified of Gaddafi's death during an interview on CBS News, then-secretary of state Hillary Clinton uttered her now infamous line, "We came, we saw, he died!"[216] The release of Clinton emails in 2016 showed evidence that she was aware of illegal extra-judicial

213   https://www.theguardian.com/us-news/2016/apr/12/barack-obama-says-libya-was-worst-mistake-of-his-presidency

214   https://edition.cnn.com/2016/06/21/politics/joe-biden-hillary-clinton-libya/index.html; https://www.latimes.com/politics/la-xpm-2011-oct-20-la-pn-santorum-kadafi-20111020-story.html

215   https://www.theatlantic.com/magazine/archive/2016/04/the-obama-doctrine/471525/

216   https://www.cbsnews.com/news/clinton-on-qaddafi-we-came-we-saw-he-died/

killings on the part of NATO-backed rebels long before many of them had taken place, and that Western special forces had trained militias suspected of having links to al-Qaeda very shortly after the first protests broke out in Benghazi in February 2011.[217]

In the seven years after the fall of Gaddafi, CNN reported, four nations conducted air strikes in Libya and hundreds of civilians died in those strikes.[218]

"So we actually executed this plan as well as I could have expected," Obama told the *Atlantic* in the 2016 interview. "We got a UN mandate, we built a coalition, it cost us $1 billion—which, when it comes to military operations, is very cheap. We averted large-scale civilian casualties, we prevented what almost surely would have been a prolonged and bloody civil conflict. And despite all that, Libya is a mess."

217 https://levantreport.com/2016/01/04/new-hillary-emails-reveal-propaganda-executions-coveting-libyan-oil-and-gold/
218 https://edition.cnn.com/2018/06/20/opinions/libya-chaos-civilian-deaths-bergen-sims/index.html

Iraq

In 2002, future vice president Joe Biden fought to launch the Iraq war from his powerful perch in the U.S. Senate Committee on Foreign Relations, which he chaired. "I do not believe this is a rush to war," Biden said a few days before the Senate voted to approve the use of military force in Iraq.[219] Biden reaffirmed his support for the war in August 2003, stating "I voted to go into Iraq, and I'd vote to do it again."[220]

Consequently, President Obama inherited a war which he spent the first half of his presidency working to withdraw from. He finally did so in 2011, when he announced that the remaining 40,000 U.S. troops in Iraq would be out by the end of the year.[221] Yet, the questionable manner in which he ultimately drew down the eight-year campaign, and his handling of the aftermath, has drawn some of the harshest criticisms of his presidency.

The timeline for the 2011 withdrawal had been determined three years beforehand by the Status of Forces Agreement put in place by the administration of George W. Bush, establishing that all U.S. combat forces would be completely out of Iraq by December 31, 2011.[222] Violations would have subjected contractors working for U.S. forces to criminal charges. Fearing dangerous destabilization, American military officials wanted to keep 20,000 to 25,000 troops in the country afterward, but that didn't happen. Noted Peter Beinart in the *Atlantic*: "Obama now claims that maintaining any residual force was impossible because Iraq's parliament would not give U.S. soldiers immunity from prosecution. Given how unpopular America's military presence was among ordinary Iraqis, that may well be true. But we can't fully know because Obama—eager to tout a full withdrawal from Iraq

219 https://www.theguardian.com/commentisfree/2020/feb/17/joe-biden-role-iraq-war
220 https://www.jacobinmag.com/2018/08/joe-biden-democratic-party-military-hawk
221 https://www.bbc.co.uk/news/av/world-us-canada-15410534
222 https://thehill.com/blogs/congress-blog/foreign-policy/315247-obamas-legacy-in-iraq

in his reelection campaign—didn't push hard to keep troops in the country."[223]

Emma Sky, former political advisor to General Ray Odierno, commanding general of U.S. forces in Iraq, elucidated the matter in her insider's account of events leading up to and following the U.S. withdrawal in a *Politico* article adapted from her book, *The Unraveling: High Hopes and Missed Opportunities in Iraq*.[224] Sky, a senior fellow at Yale University's Jackson Institute, wrote that "the seeds of Iraq's unravelling were sown in 2010, when the United States did not uphold the election results and failed to broker the formation of a new Iraqi government."

Sky painted a portrait of a supremely stymied Odierno who failed in his attempts to convince the new Obama–Biden administration of the critical need for a post-2011 stay-behind network of U.S. troops in addition to a civilian-led contingent which could train Iraqi security forces and provide the necessary psychological support. The March 2010 national election resulted in a victory for Iraqiya, a coalition headed by the secular Shia Ayad Allawi and leaders of the Sunni community, running on a non-sectarian platform. Iraqiya had won two more seats than the incumbent Maliki's State of Law Coalition. Maliki, a Shia who had been prime minister since 2006, claimed massive election fraud and demanded a recount, pushing Iraq's chief justice to reinterpret the law. Both Vice President Biden and Chris Hill, the American ambassador to Iraq, backed Maliki as prime minister, despite the vote count.

"'Why is the U.S. picking the prime minister?'" Deputy Prime Minister Rafi Issawi asked Sky. "'This is Iraq. This is our country. We have to live here. And we care passionately about building a future for our children.'"

223   https://www.theatlantic.com/international/archive/2014/06/obamas-disastrous-iraq-policy-an-autopsy/373225/

224   https://www.politico.com/magazine/story/2015/04/obama-iraq-116708

By early 2013, Maliki had detained thousands of Sunnis without trial and pushed leading Sunnis out of the political process. In April of that year, the local population of Hawija, a Sunni Arab town in northern Iraq, rose up against the government. Maliki's security forces killed more than forty civilians there. Joost Hiltermann of the International Crisis Group wrote that the event had turned the town into "a poster child for all the ills that would facilitate the Islamic State takeover one year later."[225]

In June 2013, Obama proposed 70 to 95 percent cuts in U.S. funding for Iraqi peacebuilding, human rights, and civil society.[226] The following year, he ordered U.S. troops back to Iraq to combat the ISIS insurgency, eventually authorizing "targeted airstrikes" to protect American personnel and help Iraqi forces.[227]

225 https://www.crisisgroup.org/middle-east-north-africa/gulf-and-arabian-peninsula/iraq/perils-post-isis-iraq
226 https://thehill.com/blogs/congress-blog/foreign-policy/315247-obamas-legacy-in-iraq
227 https://www.theguardian.com/world/2014/jun/17/barack-obama-sends-troops-back-to-iraq-as-crisis-worsens; https://edition.cnn.com/2014/08/07/world/iraq-options/index.html

Israel and Palestine

Palestinians and Israelis alike widely regard Obama's record at brokering peace in the region as a failure. His presidency began nonetheless with optimism on this front. In a 2009 speech at Cairo University, he called on Palestinians to renounce violence and develop a stable democratic political system.[228] In turn, he called on Israel to freeze construction of settlements in the West Bank, which Israel had captured after being attacked in the 1967 Six-Day War.

Above all, Obama's speech expressed his commitment to the objective of a fair two-state solution. But Israel rejected his call to halt construction, creating more tension between Washington and Jerusalem. Three months later, Obama quietly backed off, bitterly disappointing Palestinians.

The move set the tone for the two terms to follow. George Mitchell, a seasoned American diplomat, quit in March 2011 after two years of being special envoy to the Middle East under Obama. The previous month, Palestinian frustration and disappointment had mounted after the U.S. vetoed a U.N. Security Council resolution condemning Israeli settlements as illegal.[229] Indeed, as one report notes, "the Obama administration was the first since 1967 to block all UN Security Council resolutions that specifically criticized Israel."[230]

In 2013, early in his second term, Obama gave a speech in Jerusalem, calling on both sides to earnestly sacrifice some objectives for an equitable solution to the conflict.[231] Secretary of State John Kerry spent months in a Kissinger-like shuttle diplomacy attempt. This effort

---

228   https://obamawhitehouse.archives.gov/the-press-office/remarks-president-cairo-university-6-04-09

229   https://www.theguardian.com/world/2011/feb/19/us-veto-israel-settlement

230   https://theconversation.com/how-the-israeli-palestinian-conflict-resisted-obamas-efforts-65823

231   https://obamawhitehouse.archives.gov/the-press-office/2013/03/21/remarks-president-barack-obama-people-israel

was declared a failure by the Obama administration in March 2014. That summer an Israeli military operation in Gaza became a war, with 2,100 Palestinians killed.

The Israeli government of Benjamin Netanyahu was condemned the world over—including by a substantial proportion of the Jewish Israeli electorate—for taking harsh, unnecessary measures. The U.S. government chimed in with criticism, but in 2016 renewed an aid agreement committing the country to $38 billion in military assistance over the next ten years—the largest such aid package in U.S. history.[232] In 2017, Trump triggered global outcry by recognizing Jerusalem as Israel's capital—a move that Biden supported as much as two decades earlier as a senator.[233] A Palestinian state remains a dream. An Israel living in true peace with its Palestinian neighbors remains an ideal mired in right-wing Israeli intransigence.

232 https://www.reuters.com/article/us-usa-israel-statement/u-s-israel-sign-38-billion-military-aid-package-idUSKCN11K2CI
233 https://www.aljazeera.com/news/2020/4/29/biden-says-hed-leave-us-embassy-in-jerusalem-if-elected

Bahrain

Bahrain is a longtime ally of the United States and, in recent decades, a particularly strategic one due to its proximity to Iran. The island nation is the home of a substantial U.S. naval base, and is a vocal backer of U.S. military efforts in Afghanistan and Iraq.[234] The entrenched monarchy of Bahrain, the al-Khalifa family, has awarded many American companies lucrative defense and other types of contracts.

The ruling family has exerted consistent pressure on domestic democracy advocates in recent years, including through the use of torture.[235] With rising inequality between Bahrain's impoverished Shiite majority and its better-off Sunni minority, the government has implemented brutal putdowns of dissidents such as evidenced in its response to widespread pro-democracy riots in February 2011, which saw security forces firing live rounds into crowds.[236] Protesters were routinely injured and killed with U.S.-provided weapons, with the Obama administration approving $200 million in arms sales to Bahrain in 2010, months before the crackdown.[237] Many others are currently detained and face court martial proceedings.[238]

President Obama issued a public criticism of Bahrain's use of violence against the democracy protestors, but Bahrain's continued brutal repression of its own citizens throughout 2011 and beyond elicited no further U.S. action.[239] Shortly after a June 2011 meeting with Bahraini

234   https://www.thebalanceeveryday.com/installation-overview-nsa-bahrain-kingdom-of-bahrain-3354695; https://worldview.stratfor.com/article/bahrains-importance-united-states

235   https://www.independent.co.uk/news/world/middle-east/power-struggle-deepens-divisions-among-bahraini-royal-family-2361462.html

236   https://www.hrw.org/news/2011/02/18/bahrain-army-police-fire-protesters

237   https://www.aljazeera.com/news/2011/06/11/us-arms-sales-to-bahrain-surged-in-2010/

238   https://www.hrw.org/news/2020/02/25/nine-years-after-bahrains-uprising-its-human-rights-crisis-has-only-worsened#

239   https://obamawhitehouse.archives.gov/the-press-office/2011/05/19/remarks-president-middle-east-and-north-africa; https://www.amnesty.org/en/latest/

Crown Prince Salman bin Hamad al-Khalifa, Obama affirmed that America was a "close friend of Bahrain", a friendship that was further emphasized after Bahrain ordered $53 million of armaments from the U.S.[240]

In 2016, after five years of popular unrest, the well-known dissident Nabeel Rajab, who spoke regularly of torture in Bahrain's prisons, was himself sentenced to a prolonged prison term.[241] All the while, the Obama administration failed to defend democratic values in Bahrain, even though the U.S. was (and remains) by far the most influential Western country in the region.

news/2013/04/bahrains-dark-side-empty-promises-while-repression-goes-unabated/

240 https://obamawhitehouse.archives.gov/the-press-office/2011/09/21/remarks-president-obama-address-united-nations-general-assembly; https://foreignpolicy.com/2011/10/05/congress-gears-up-to-fight-arms-sales-to-bahrain/; https://foreignpolicy.com/2012/01/27/obama-administration-using-loophole-to-quietly-sell-arms-package-to-bahrain/; https://uk.reuters.com/article/us-usa-bahrain/u-s-resumes-bahrain-arms-sales-despite-rights-concerns-idUSBRE84A11R20120512

241 https://www.aljazeera.com/news/2018/01/16/bahrain-ruling-on-nabeel-rajab-jail-term-condemned/

Egypt

On the day that Vice President Joe Biden praised the Arab Spring as a "democratic movement" during a June 2012 Virginia high school commencement address, the Egyptian high court nullified the Islamist majority parliament and the Egyptian military assumed control of the legislature.[242] "The democratic movement that swept across the Middle East, the so-called Arab Spring, began when a lowly fruit vendor set himself ablaze to protest a corrupt government, igniting a confrontation magnified by social media that literally set off a revolution that was waiting to happen for well over 200 years," Biden told the students.

The following year, Egyptian general Abdel Fattah el-Sisi seized power in a military coup, overthrowing the democratically elected successor to Hosni Mubarak, Mohamed Morsi. Sisi proceeded to arrest thousands of citizens. He carried out a bloodbath, ordering his security forces to mow down one thousand pro-Morsi demonstrators conducting a sit-in.[243] The massacre was historically uncommon, even by Egypt's brutal standards.

At the time, President Obama expressed shock and indignation over the mass killing, and the palpable sincerity of his feelings came through in his condemnations. "We can't return to business as usual," he insisted. "We have to be very careful about being seen as aiding and abetting actions that we think run contrary to our values and ideals."[244]

With that and similar statements, Obama halted the delivery of Harpoon missiles, F-16's, and attack helicopters. He stopped the

---

242 https://cnsnews.com/news/article/biden-praises-arab-spring-same-day-egypt-dissolves-its-parliament; https://obamawhitehouse.archives.gov/the-press-office/2012/06/14/remarks-vice-president-joe-biden-tallwood-high-school-graduation-ceremon

243 https://www.hrw.org/report/2014/08/12/all-according-plan/raba-massacre-and-mass-killings-protesters-egypt

244 https://www.politico.com/magazine/story/2016/01/we-caved-obama-foreign-policy-legacy-213495

transfer of $260 million in cash to the Egyptian government and expressed doubts over the continuation of $1.3 billion in annual transfers to the Egyptian military.

A number of Obama's top advisors split off from his view and the views of the advisors in sync with him. They argued vociferously that cutting off supplies of military hardware or cash to Egypt would be a huge strategic error. Moreover, Sisi thumbed his nose repeatedly at the administration when it sought his assistance in the region.

Finally, Obama succumbed to both Egyptian and domestic advisory pressure. In March 2015, Obama called the dictator, promising to release the cash transfers and the hardware, and assured him that the annual $1.3 billion in military cash assistance would continue.[245] He kept his promise.

245 https://www.theguardian.com/us-news/2015/mar/31/obama-restores-us-military-aid-to-egypt

Syria

On August 20, 2012, President Obama was asked at a White House press corps briefing what could prompt him to use military force in President Bashar al-Assad's violence-infested Syria. "We have been very clear to the Assad regime, but also to other players on the ground, that a red line for us is we start seeing a whole bunch of chemical weapons moving around or being utilized," Obama responded.[246] "That would change my calculus." One year later, almost to the day, more than 1,400 people were killed allegedly by Syrian forces in a sarin gas attack in the Damascus suburb of Ghouta.[247]

Yet, Obama backed off his now infamous "red line" comment, keeping U.S. forces out of Syria for the duration of his administration, later attributing the decision largely to uneasiness over a lack of support from Congress, the American public, and the international community. Consequently, the mayhem escalated. Since the start of the Syrian Civil War in 2011, at least half a million people have been killed and more than half the population has been displaced.[248] It was widely felt that Obama's approach damaged U.S. credibility throughout the world.

"How did a man who took office espousing a new era of engagement with the world end up a spectator to this century's greatest humanitarian catastrophe?" Barbara Plett Usher, a BBC State Department correspondent, wondered in a piece analyzing Obama's tepid response to the situation.[249] Explaining away his position in a 2016 press conference, Obama said military intervention would have been impossible to do "on the cheap."[250] But, according to Usher, some senior military

246 https://obamawhitehouse.archives.gov/the-press-office/2012/08/20/remarks-president-white-house-press-corps
247 https://www.bbc.co.uk/news/world-middle-east-23927399
248 https://www.syriahr.com/en/157193/
249 https://www.bbc.co.uk/news/world-us-canada-38297343
250 https://www.theguardian.com/us-news/2016/dec/16/obama-syria-assad-aleppo-final-press-conference

and cabinet officials had vociferously disagreed, arguing in favor of a limited engagement rather than a mass ground deployment to tilt the balance of power against Assad.

Wall Street Journal reporter Jay Solomon shed some additional light on Obama's "calculus" in his book, *The Iran Wars*. "When the president announced his plans to attack [the Assad regime] and then pulled back, it was exactly the period in time when American negotiators were meeting with Iranian negotiators secretly in Oman to get the nuclear agreement," Solomon told MSNBC in 2016.[251] "US and Iranian officials have both told me that they were basically communicating that if the U.S. starts hitting President Assad's forces, Iran's closest Arab ally [...] these talks cannot conclude." Ned Price, spokesman for the White House's National Security Council, denied the claim.

251   https://www.msnbc.com/andrea-mitchell-reports/watch/inside-the-us-iran-struggle-748574275947

Cuba

On December 17, 2014, U.S. President Barack Obama and Cuban President Raúl Castro announced their joint intention to normalize relations between the two countries. The agreements they forged over the next year and a half included an end to most U.S. travel restrictions, as well as fewer impediments to Americans who wished to send money to Cuba. U.S. banks were granted entrée into the Cuban banking system and the embassies of both nations were to be opened to the public and operated as full-service diplomatic outposts.

This delicate process ended a fifty-five-year stretch of overt hostility between the two countries. For much of this time, Cuba had been under the strategic thumb of the now-defunct Soviet Union. Some months after the thawing was announced, Obama stated his intention to rescind Cuba's designation as a State Sponsor of Terrorism, and indeed he did so, on May 29, 2015.[252] These steps toward normalization culminated in his March 2016 trip to Cuba, which was the first visit there by a U.S. president since 1928.[253]

But scarcely more than a year later, after U.S. personnel in Cuba began to report mysterious health ailments, President Trump unceremoniously declared a cancellation of all the Obama era's agreements with Cuba. On June 16, 2017, Trump, who had promised during his campaign to cut ties with Cuba, declared that the U.S. was giving away too much in exchange for too little.[254] A few months later, due to what appeared to be ongoing sonic harassment of U.S. Embassy employees, Trump ordered most of the diplomats in Cuba to return home.[255] He also evicted Cuban diplomats from their embassy in the United States.

---

252 https://obamawhitehouse.archives.gov/blog/2015/05/29/rescission-cuba-state-sponsor-terrorism

253 https://www.nytimes.com/interactive/projects/cp/international/obama-in-cuba

254 https://www.theatlantic.com/news/archive/2017/06/trump-cuba-policy/530514/

255 https://theconversation.com/is-trump-using-health-attacks-on-us-diplomats-in-havana-as-an-excuse-to-punish-cuba-85163; https://eu.usatoday.com/story/news/

Afghanistan

Major American military involvement in the Afghanistan War began in 2001 and continues to this day. It is the longest war in American history. More than 2,400 Americans have lost their lives fighting in Afghanistan, and $2,000,000,000,000 (two trillion dollars) has been spent by the U.S. on this conflict.[256] This is a very large sum indeed, amounting to $15,500 for every American household. In Afghanistan, a nation in which per capita gross domestic product was only $502 in 2019, this would amount to $52,573 or one hundred consecutive years' worth of income for every man, woman, and child.[257]

At the end of 2014, total U.S. expenditure on the War in Afghanistan amounted to $1 trillion, about 80 percent of which was under the first five years of Obama's presidency.[258] Just where all that money went is unknown, as no adequate audit has ever been conducted. John Sopko, then-special inspector general for Afghanistan reconstruction, said that "billions of dollars" of funds were stolen or wasted on projects that often made little sense for the conditions in Afghanistan.[259] But occasionally, particular boondoggles have been revealed, such as the 2015 watchdog report on a gas station that cost $43 million to build, and still was not finished.[260]

The staggering cost of this unresolved conflict is dwarfed not only by the number of Americans killed, but by the tens of thousands who have suffered severe injuries, each of them heart-rending. The number of American soldiers killed during Obama's terms of office was nearly

world/2018/03/02/u-s-makes-staff-cuts-embassy-cuba-permanent/389532002/

256 https://www.nytimes.com/interactive/2019/12/09/world/middleeast/afghanistan-war-cost.html

257 https://data.worldbank.org/indicator/NY.GDP.PCAP.CD?locations=AF

258 https://www.cnbc.com/2014/12/15/-for-us-cost-1tn.html

259 https://www.cnbc.com/2014/12/15/-for-us-cost-1tn.html

260 https://www.cnbc.com/2015/11/02/us-spent-43-million-on-afghanistan-gas-station-watchdog-report.html

triple the number killed during the George W. Bush administration.[261] More than 38,000 Afghan civilians were killed in the conflict between 2001 and 2018.[262]

At the time of America's entry into the war under George W. Bush, according to the Defense Department, the Taliban controlled zero percent of Afghanistan. However, by the final months of Obama's second term, the Taliban controlled 30 percent.[263] This is hardly progress.

Another measure of the futility of this war is that more than 80 percent of the world's opium currently comes from Afghanistan.[264] The area of opium cultivation climbed from 123,000 hectares to over 200,000 during the Obama administration.[265]

In his first few years in office, Obama boosted the number of American soldiers in Afghanistan more than threefold, from around 30,000 to more than 100,000 in 2011.[266] The intention was to disrupt the Taliban, train Afghan security forces to defend their own country, and strengthen the government before a withdrawal by the end of Obama's second term.

The move lacked the support of Vice President Biden, who warned Obama that the rationale behind it was flawed, according to a book by *Washington Post* correspondent Rajiv Chandrasekaran. The book, *Little America: The War Within the War for Afghanistan,* revealed a November 2009 memo from Biden to Obama, in which the vice president expressed doubts about whether the same counterinsurgency

261   https://www.statista.com/statistics/262894/western-coalition-soldiers-killed-in-afghanistan/
262   https://www.nytimes.com/interactive/2019/12/09/world/middleeast/afghanistan-war-cost.html
263   https://www.politico.com/magazine/story/2016/10/afghanistan-longest-war-next-president-214324
264   https://wdr.unodc.org/wdr2020/field/WDR20_Booklet_3.pdf
265   https://www.unodc.org/documents/crop-monitoring/Afghanistan/AfghanistanOpiumSurvey2016_ExSum.pdf
266   https://www.npr.org/2016/07/06/484979294/chart-how-the-u-s-troop-levels-in-afghanistan-have-changed-under-obama

strategy that had been used in Iraq could be successful in Afghanistan. Referring to a White House review of the war, Biden wrote, "I do not see how anyone who took part in our discussions could emerge without profound questions about the viability of counterinsurgency." [267] He advocated instead for a buildup of 20,000 troops (half the number requested by then-war commander General Stanley McChrystal), to be paired with a "credible" Afghan government and Afghan security services that could take over. Obama struck an apparent compromise, sending in 30,000 troops at the time.

At the beginning of 2014, Biden pushed for almost all troops to be removed by the end of the year.[268] This approach was consistent with his counterterrorism strategy, which emphasized a few thousand troops to train the Afghan Army, paired with C.I.A. drones and Special Ops units to hunt down terrorists.

To his credit, by the end of his presidency, Obama had reduced the number of troops in Afghanistan by over two-thirds from the time he took office. However, the drawdown didn't work out quite that well. A mere few months into Donald Trump's presidency, with the Taliban proving tougher to beat back than expected, his secretary of defense decided to send 3,500 fresh troops to join the 11,000 already in Afghanistan, claiming the number at the end of Obama's tenure was inadequate.[269]

267 https://www.syracuse.com/news/2012/06/joe_biden_in_leaked_memo_told.html
268 https://www.wsj.com/articles/biden-seeks-deep-cut-in-us-afghan-force-1389918441
269 https://thehill.com/policy/defense/349486-us-to-send-3500-more-troops-to-afghanistan-report

North Korea

As strategic studies scholar Mark Fitzpatrick put it, North Korea was the biggest blemish on President Obama's non-proliferation record.[270] During his time in office, North Korea conducted four nuclear tests and carried out more than fifty missile and rocket launches. It had the capacity to rain nuclear warheads on its neighbors and was well within reach of the U.S. with its nuclear weaponry by the time Obama left office.

Early in Obama's presidency, North Korea introduced a uranium enrichment program, which complemented its plutonium production. It also tested submarine-launched payloads, intermediate-range Musudan missiles, and satellite-launch rockets appropriate for intercontinental-range missiles. At the same time, it insisted it would not relinquish membership in the nuclear club. The six-party talks intended to end North Korea's nuclear program were moribund, having last been held prior to Obama taking office.

Obama employed what has generally been described as a "strategic patience" approach to North Korea, in reference to a 2015 national security paper in which he stated that "the challenges we face require strategic patience and persistence."[271]

"The Obama administration's approach to North Korea was a failure," said Kelsey Davenport, director for non-proliferation policy at the Arms Control Association.[272] "If anything, it gave North Korea time to continue to advance its nuclear missile programs."

The administration's demand that North Korea move toward denuclearization before Obama even demonstrated willingness to

---

270 https://www.armscontrol.org/act/2016-11/features/north-korea-obama%E2%80%99 99s-prime-nonproliferation-failure

271 https://obamawhitehouse.archives.gov/sites/default/files/docs/2015_national_ security_strategy_2.pdf

272 https://www.dw.com/en/why-donald-trump-was-right-about-barack-obamas-north-korea-policy/a-40230149

engage in talks, was "putting the cart before the horse," according to Davenport. "It required North Korea to commit to the end state of negotiations and take steps toward that without the U.S. committing to anything." In addition, she called the preconditions for negotiations "onerous and excessive," and said the administration's sanctions policy was carried out haphazardly.

"By pretty much any measure, strategic patience was a failure," agreed Celeste Arrington, a Korea expert at George Washington University, who called the Obama stance toward North Korea "reactive and passive."[273] She added: "Maybe the Obama administration could have pushed more forcefully for dialogue or tried to get back to the 2005 and 2006 six-party talks."

In both 2014 and 2015, Davenport noted, North Korea offered to freeze nuclear missile tests in return for a freeze on U.S.–South Korean military exercises, but Washington did not seriously consider the offer. "When North Korea opened the door for talks, the United States quickly shut it again," she said.

273 https://www.dw.com/en/why-donald-trump-was-right-about-barack-obamas-north-korea-policy/a-40230149

China

Pointing to laws it says were enacted "under the guise of 'national security,'" a 2018 report by Amnesty International enumerated widespread human rights violations in China.[274] Nobel Peace Prize laureate and outspoken government critic Liu Xiaobo died in custody in 2017 after several years of incarceration. Activists, advocates, and protesters were sentenced on charges like "picking quarrels" and "provoking trouble." Police detained human rights activists for long stretches in buildings that were not officially for detention, in some cases without access to loved ones or counsel. Strict controls on internet usage were implemented. Religious repression was widespread unless a church proved itself to be straight-down-the-line loyal to the regime in Beijing. "Counter-terrorism" and "anti-separatism" campaigns flourished and were particularly harsh in the Xinjiang Uighur Autonomous Region and in Tibetan-populated areas. And Hong Kong came under freedom of expression attacks, as the "government used vague and overbroad charges to prosecute pro-democracy activists."

When Chinese President Xi Jinping arrived in Washington on an official visit in 2015, he was greeted with a twenty-one gun salute and a champagne-drenched state dinner. While public figures urged President Obama to openly address human rights with Xi, this wasn't taken on as a significant topic.

At an earlier meeting with Chinese leadership, Obama had suggested that China be held to a lower human rights standard than other countries. He insisted: "China has a different political system than we do. China is at a different stage of development than we are. We come from very different cultures with very different histories."[275]

274 https://www.amnesty.org/download/Documents/POL1067002018ENGLISH.PDF
275 https://www.politico.com/story/2015/09/xi-humanrights-213999

Obama visited China three times during his presidency. On his final visit, in 2016, the *New York Times* reported that "human rights barely registered" in his discussions with the Chinese leadership.[276]

Assessing his human rights record in 2017, the journal *Foreign Policy* criticized Obama for failing "to develop anything remotely like a strategy to support those across China struggling to defend basic freedoms. During his interactions with senior Chinese leaders, he offered only minimal, abstract comments on human rights, rarely calling publicly even for the release of people like his fellow Nobel Peace Prize laureate Liu Xiaobo."[277]

276 https://www.nytimes.com/2016/09/08/world/asia/obama-asia-human-rights.html
277 https://foreignpolicy.com/2017/01/04/barack-obamas-shaky-legacy-on-human-rights/

Special Ops

A memo emailed by the Defense Department's office of security review to Pentagon staff members in March 2009 advised that the Obama administration preferred to avoid using the term "Long War" or "Global War on Terror," in favor of "Overseas Contingency Operation," reported the *Washington Post*.[278]

Whatever it was called, increasing numbers of U.S. Special Operations troops were deployed to take part in it during the Obama years. Special Ops recruitment saw a marked rise beginning in the post–9/11 Bush era and continuing through the end of the Obama presidency. In 2001, according to the *New York Times*, the number of Special Ops personnel—including soldiers, civilians, National Guard, and Reservists—was 45,600. In 2011, it had grown to 61,400 and, in 2016, to 70,000.[279]

"To his critics, Obama's embrace of special operations forces looks exactly like the Bush-era 'global war on terror' that he was supposed to have rejected," declared MSNBC in 2014.[280] Even as the numbers continued to creep up that year, Admiral William H. McRaven, then head of Special Operations Command (Socom), told Congress that "the force has continued to fray" from endless deployment cycles, prompting the Army alone to put out a call for 5,000 new Special Ops candidates.[281]

"While most defense and intelligence activities are drawing down, and their budgets are declining, investment in special operations is on the rise," Steven Aftergood, head of the Project on Government Secrecy at the Federation of American Scientists told MSNBC.

278 https://www.washingtonpost.com/wp-dyn/content/article/2009/03/24/AR2009032402818.html

279 https://www.nytimes.com/2016/01/31/opinion/sunday/welcome-to-the-age-of-the-commando.html

280 https://www.msnbc.com/msnbc/obama-embraces-special-operations-forces-msna351736

281 https://www.nytimes.com/2016/01/31/opinion/sunday/welcome-to-the-age-of-the-commando.html

In 2015, Secretary of Defense Ashton B. Carter announced at a House hearing that a "specialized expeditionary targeting force" would be sent to Iraq to conduct raids on top Islamic State targets.[282] It would join the 3,500 troops already there working as advisers and trainers.

Military analysts took heed when the Obama DoD announced in early 2016 that General Joseph Votel, who headed U.S. Special Operations Forces (SOF), was to take over U.S. Central Command, a position that had traditionally gone to a general of more conventional background, and a first for a career Green Beret officer. It was considered a sign of Obama's trust in, and reliance on Special Operations, wrote Matt Gallagher, a former Army captain and Iraq war veteran, in the *New York Times*.[283] "In the political sense, the policy works," Gallagher added. "The secrecy surrounding Special Ops keeps the heavy human costs of war off the front pages. But in doing so, it also keeps the nonmilitary public wholly disconnected from the armed violence carried out in our name. It enables our state of perpetual warfare, and ensures that as little as we care and understand today, we'll care and understand even less tomorrow."

A few months later, Obama announced that an additional 250 Special Ops forces would be sent to Syria. Rather than leading a fight on the ground, he said during a speech in Hanover, Germany, the troops would be training and assisting local forces. "So, make no mistake, these terrorists will learn the same lesson as others before them have, which is 'your hatred is no match for our nations united in the defense of our way of life,'" he said.[284]

---

282 https://www.washingtonpost.com/world/national-security/new-iraq-task-force-expands-direct-us-role-in-battle-against-islamic-state/2015/12/01/6cc41ef2-9861-11e5-8917-653b65c809eb_story.html

283 https://www.nytimes.com/2016/01/31/opinion/sunday/welcome-to-the-age-of-the-commando.html

284 https://edition.cnn.com/2016/04/24/politics/obama-special-operations-syria/index.html

At the end of Obama's term in January 2017, U.S. Special Ops forces were deployed to 138 nations, 70 percent of the world's countries, according to figures supplied to TomDispatch by U.S. Special Operations Command.[285]

285 https://www.thenation.com/article/archive/american-special-forces-are-deployed-to-70-percent-of-the-worlds-countries/

Yemen

A September 2016 report found that Obama had offered Saudi Arabia $115 billion in weapons, in aggregate, since coming into office.[286] Given that, as a general arms industry rule of thumb, the vast majority of offers turn into contractual agreements—that is, sales—this was invariably a huge bonanza for the arms industry.

In early 2015, the Shia Houthi of northern Yemen, who for decades had fought the government of President Ali Abdullah Saleh, went on to rapidly take over the national capital, Sana'a. The takeover was facilitated partly by a newly forged alliance of convenience the Houthi had struck with Saleh, who had been forced out of power during a 2011 Arab Spring uprising.[287] The U.S., Saudi Arabia's ally, feared Iranian involvement in the attacks, despite a lack of direct evidence.[288]

The Saudis, heavily armed with sophisticated weaponry —a result of massive American arms sales by the Obama administration, as well as others previous to his—partnered with forces loyal to the incumbent president, Abd-Rabbu Mansour Hadi, in order to fight off the Houthi onslaught. Outfitted with cutting-edge weaponry purchased from the Americans, and fueled by a fear of Iranian expansionism, the Kingdom of Saudi Arabia and its Gulf allies started airstrikes against the Houthi on March 26, 2015.

In September 2016, during his final speech as president of the United States to the United Nations General Assembly, Obama betrayed a deep pessimism with regard to ending ethnic and religious conflict.[289] This was understandable, given the more than

---

286 http://securityassistance.org/fact_sheet/us-arms-transfers-saudi-arabia-and-war-yemen

287 https://www.amnesty.org/en/latest/news/2015/09/yemen-the-forgotten-war/

288 https://www.theatlantic.com/international/archive/2016/09/yemen-saudi-arabia-obama-riyadh/501365/

289 https://obamawhitehouse.archives.gov/the-press-office/2016/09/20/address-president-obama-71st-session-united-nations-general-assembly

10,000 who were killed in the Yemen civil war over the previous year and a half.[290]

A day after the UN speech, the U.S. Senate debated a resolution that would have blocked the sale of another batch of arms to Saudi Arabia, this time a $1.15-billion package that included 153 Abrams tanks. The *Atlantic* described the package as "a drop in the bucket."[291] The sale went through.

It is almost inconceivable as to why a nation of 30 million people would need over $100 billion in state-of-the-art ordnance and related items in addition to the hundreds of billions worth purchased in years prior. One hundred billion dollars is more than what every country on the face of the planet, excepting the United States and China, spends on its entire annual defense budget.

The $1.15 billion in sales, eighteen months into Saudi Arabia's entrance into the conflict, led many observers, for or against the sale, to conclude that it represented the Obama administration's affirmation of clear intent to continue its role in what the *Atlantic* summed up as "a deadly, strategically incoherent war." From the moment Saudi King Salman announced his intervention in Yemen, the Obama administration was there, organizing intelligence-sharing operations and logistical assistance, such as aerial refueling.

Diplomatic attempts by the Obama administration, such as Secretary of State John Kerry's forays into the conflict, came to naught. Obama is yet "to acknowledge his culpability for what the United Nations calls the world's worst ongoing humanitarian catastrophe or to try to publicly atone for it."[292]

290 https://www.aljazeera.com/news/2016/08/30/un-at-least-10000-killed-in-yemen-conflict/

291 https://www.theatlantic.com/international/archive/2016/09/yemen-saudi-arabia-obama-riyadh/501365/

292 https://www.huffingtonpost.co.uk/entry/biden-obama-saudi-arabia-yemen_n_5df14e46e4b0b75fb53702c3

Iran Deal

During his two terms as president, Obama took it upon himself to secure the freedom of four Americans who were held against their will by the Iranian government. He was successful in this endeavor but, in the end, he used the carrot more than the stick.

Some months after the four American prisoners were released in January 2016, the *Wall Street Journal* reported that the Obama administration had surreptitiously airdropped into Iran wooden pallets stacked with $400 million in foreign banknotes.[293] Obama responded in a news conference at the Pentagon that the $400 million airdrop had nothing to do with the prisoners' release, even though it took place on the same day.[294] Rather, he said, it had to do with the U.S. unfreezing some Iranian assets during talks that were held simultaneously with the hostage talks. These assets had been in dispute for decades and were being contested before an international tribunal.[295] The hostages were not at issue at the tribunal hearings.

Eventually, another $1.3 billion of the decades-old contested assets was delivered to Iran, for a grand total of $1.7 billion handed over by the U.S.[296] A payment of cash to a foreign entity for forcibly held Americans would be in contravention of the United States' non-payment of ransom policy.

As a result of the *Wall Street Journal* breaking the cash drop story, much of the media took a skeptical view of Obama's insistence that the release of the hostages had nothing to do with the payout, and that it was a mere coincidence. Then-presidential candidate Donald Trump attacked this putative quid pro quo as a sign of weakness.

---

293 https://www.wsj.com/articles/u-s-sent-cash-to-iran-as-americans-were-freed-1470181874

294 https://www.reuters.com/article/us-usa-iran-installment-obama-idUSKCN10F2MH

295 https://www.vox.com/2016/9/7/12830688/us-iran-cash-payment-ransom

296 https://www.wsj.com/articles/u-s-sent-two-more-planeloads-of-cash-to-iran-after-initial-payment-1473208256

Also under Obama, and much more significantly, the U.S., along with six other world military powers, reached an agreement with Iran on its nuclear policy in July 2015.[297] In exchange for Iran agreeing to suspend its enriched uranium and plutonium programs, the U.S. and its partners agreed to lift financial- and oil-related sanctions that had been imposed on the country for pursuing these programs.

According to Tzvi Kahn, senior policy analyst at the Foreign Policy Initiative, both "deals" were a failure. As Kahn explained, "The $400 million payment, which Tehran has transferred to its military, directly subsidizes Iran's hegemonic ambitions [. . .] It has led the regime to capture more hostages. And it demonstrates that the nuclear deal, far from moderating Iran, has merely emboldened it to further provoke America, secure in the knowledge that the White House will do almost anything to protect its signature foreign policy achievement."[298]

297   https://www.vox.com/2018/5/8/17319608/trump-iran-nuclear-deal-announcement-explained
298   https://www.salon.com/2016/08/04/republicans_were_right_the_iran_deal_is_a_travesty_and_obama_is_to_blame

Burma

In late November 2016, John McKissick, head of the UN refugee agency UNHCR in the Bangladeshi border town of Cox's Bazar, gave official weight to something that had been alleged for weeks. According to McKissick, a program of ethnic cleansing was being carried out in the western Burmese state of Arakan against the country's Islamic minority, the Rohingya.

Specifically, government troops had been "killing men, shooting them, slaughtering children, raping women, burning and looting houses," and forcing them into neighboring Bangladesh, McKissick said.[299] There were refugee camps for the Rohingya in desperately poor Bangladesh, but since they were not recognized as refugees by the Bangladeshi government, many were forcibly returned to Burma. The Burmese government denied reports of the atrocities.

A little more than a week after the UNHCR announcement, President Obama lifted government aid sanctions against Burma (also known as Myanmar), stating that the authorities there had shown "substantial progress in improving human rights."[300] The *New York Times*, quoting Obama, added that these sanctions were lifted "even though the country's army is in the midst of a brutal campaign to drive out the Rohingya."

Obama had already indicated he hoped to bring about improvements in the human rights situation in Burma by using a carrot approach of eliminating certain bilateral trade restrictions that had long been imposed on the country by the United States. But experts widely viewed the November 2016 policy adjustment as inept and premature. John Sifton, Asia policy director for Human Rights Watch, called the decision "astounding."

299 https://www.aljazeera.com/news/2016/11/25/rohingya-face-myanmar-ethnic-cleansing-un-official/

300 https://www.nytimes.com/2016/12/02/us/politics/obama-lifts-sanctions-myanmar.html

Bomber

During Barack Obama's eight-year tenure as president, U.S.-led forces dropped approximately 100,000 bombs and missiles on seven countries, surpassing the 70,000 dropped on five countries during George W. Bush's equally long presidency.[301] In 2016, Obama's final full year as commander in chief, his military dropped at least 26,171 bombs on foreign countries.[302]

The woeful statistic—an average of almost three bombs an hour, twenty-four hours a day, for every day in 2016—inevitably summoned memories of the auspicious occasion seven years earlier, when Obama was awarded the 2009 Nobel Peace Prize. He was lauded for his "extraordinary efforts to strengthen international diplomacy and cooperation between peoples."[303]

The victims of the 2016 bombings were both combatants and civilians. Most of the air attacks took place in Syria and Iraq, but the bombs also struck Afghanistan, Libya, Yemen, Somalia, and Pakistan, seven Muslim-majority countries.

According to the Council on Foreign Relations, the figure of 26,171 bombs was "an undoubtedly low estimate," as reliable data was available for airstrikes in only four of the countries, and, according to the Pentagon's definition, a single strike can involve multiple bombs or munitions. It still meant that the United States dropped 3,028 more bombs—and in one additional country, Libya—in 2016 than it did in 2015. Moreover, CFR research also showed that the U.S. dropped 79 percent of all 30,743 coalition bombs in 2016.

Obama entered office pledging to end George W. Bush's wars. Instead, he authorized a dramatic expansion of U.S. air wars and use of special operations forces around the globe.

---

301   https://consortiumnews.com/2017/01/18/obamas-bombing-legacy/
302   https://www.cfr.org/blog/how-many-bombs-did-united-states-drop-2016
303   https://www.nobelprize.org/prizes/peace/2009/summary/

Nuclear Arms Modernization

Obama began his presidency proclaiming his intention to do away with nuclear arms once and for all.[304] But by the end of his second term, this idea had been replaced with a vow to build up the nuclear stockpile and modernize nuclear production facilities at a total cost of $1 trillion over thirty years.[305] This sum, an estimate based on Obama's 2016 budget request, included expenditures to redesign warheads for missiles, bombers, and submarines. Why the about-face?

Of all the disappointments to progressives wrought by the Obama–Biden administration, this trillion-dollar earmark vies for most egregious. The United States possesses more than six thousand nuclear warheads today, enough to destroy humanity several times over.[306] Yet modernization is decreed a priority—a modernization, mind you, that flagrantly violates the Nuclear Non-Proliferation Treaty.[307]

The proposed redesigned weapons, with their expensive delivery systems, would be inefficient and potentially completely ineffective—for example, in defending against a nuclear device in a shipping container set to dock at a domestic port, or a nuke smuggled across the Mexican border in a backpack.

As the *Intercept* reported in 2016, "President Obama's defense budget request for 2017 includes language that makes it clear that nuclear 'modernization' really is about Russia after all. The budget request explicitly cites Russian aggression, saying, 'We are countering

---

304 https://www.theguardian.com/world/2009/apr/05/nuclear-weapons-barack-obama

305 https://billmoyers.com/story/the-trillion-dollar-question-the-media-have-neglected-to-ask-presidential-candidates/; https://www.armscontrol.org/blog/2016-02-09/last-obama-budget-goes-broke-nuclear-weapons

306 https://fas.org/issues/nuclear-weapons/status-world-nuclear-forces/

307 https://www.armscontrol.org/act/2014-05/nuclear-weapons-modernization-threat-npt

Russia's aggressive policies through investments in a broad range of capabilities ... [including] our nuclear arsenal.'"[308]

Vigilance focused on securing our borders from attack by any means should be our watchword, but it is worth reflecting on the absurdity of expanding our nuclear arsenal in an ever-more interdependent world, one where our adversaries are also our partners and have trillions invested in our economy. This foreign-owned capital is in the form of plant and equipment, real estate, and intellectual property, all of which are owned by potential attackers, who would be destroying all these assets situated on American soil that they themselves have purchased. Likewise, is it sensible to further build up our nuclear stockpile when we ourselves own some of the overseas assets that would be destroyed should we launch an attack?

A nightmare conflagration risks the unthinkable—the irradiation of millions on both sides. Why? To transform productive assets into irradiated junk. To "take over" irradiated territory. To physically destroy trillions in productive facilities on their respective opposing side's territory. What does winning look like?

308 https://theintercept.com/2016/02/23/obamas-new-rationale-for-1-trillion-nuclear-program-augurs-a-new-arms-race-with-russia/

F-35

When the F-35 Lightning II Joint Strike Fighter jet program officially began in 2001, the aircraft was billed as a replacement for several aging airplane types. It was touted as being two decades ahead, technologically, of any potential adversary's creation. Despite the exaggerated claims, the F-35 has failed to meet many of its design objectives at an almost unfathomable total cost of $1.5 trillion.[309] It is the most expensive program in world history. The cost per airplane, above $100 million, is twice the initial estimate.

An article in the *Conversation* quoted Hugh Harkins, an acclaimed expert on combat aircraft, as stating that, "the F-35 cannot compete with the [Russian] Su-35S for out-and-out performance, such as speed, climb, altitude, and maneuverability."[310] The article also quoted from Air Force veteran and historian Robert Dorr's book, *Air Power Abandoned*, in which he concluded that "the F-35 demonstrates repeatedly that it can't live up to promises made for it. ... it's that bad."

Pierre Sprey, a well-known defense analyst, casually referred to the F-35 as a "turkey" and, more pointedly, lambasted it as "inherently a terrible airplane."[311] Sprey argued that "the F-35 would likely lose a close-in combat encounter to a well-flown MiG-21," the 1950s-design Soviet fighter, and that the real mission of the airplane is for the U.S. Congress to spend money with the defense contractor Lockheed Martin.

In 2014, the program was seven years behind schedule and $163 billion over budget. The Pentagon, however, "simply plunged ahead."[312] As late as 2017, the Defense Department said that the outgoing Obama

309 https://www.thenation.com/article/archive/f35-fighter-jet-pentagon/
310 https://theconversation.com/what-went-wrong-with-the-f-35-lockheed-martins-joint-strike-fighter-60905
311 https://theconversation.com/what-went-wrong-with-the-f-35-lockheed-martins-joint-strike-fighter-60905
312 https://www.thenation.com/article/archive/f35-fighter-jet-pentagon/

administration remained confident in the capabilities of the flawed multi-mission aircraft. Nevertheless, with the F-35 program now a decade behind schedule, many experienced voices continued to call for its immediate cancellation, or at the very least, serious adjustments, regardless of sunk costs.

One voice was that of the director of weapons testing at the Pentagon, who warned the incoming Trump administration to rigorously and comprehensively conduct reviews of the F-35 program. He said that the program was at high risk of sacrificing essential combat performance if the problems with the jet were not corrected.

In 2019, the *Nation* commented that, "As ephemeral as the F-35 stealth fighter may prove in historical terms, it's already a classic symbol of America's ever more fruitless forever wars. Like them, the F-35 program has proven staggeringly expensive, incredibly wasteful, and impossible to stop, no matter the woeful results. It has come to symbolize the too-big-to-fail, too-sacrosanct-to-reject part of America's militarized culture of technological violence."[313]

For the F-35, the Obama years were full steam ahead, and a veritable bonanza for military contractors.

---

313   https://www.thenation.com/article/archive/f35-fighter-jet-pentagon/

Gitmo

On the coast of Guantánamo Bay in Cuba is a small American enclave, the Guantánamo Bay Naval Base, known colloquially as Gitmo, home to an eponymous detention center. Housing male prisoners sentenced for indefinite periods of time, it has been termed a human rights abomination by Amnesty International. President Obama heartily shared this opinion, and after repeatedly promising to do so during his first presidential campaign, he issued an executive order on his second day in office to padlock the institution within a year. At the time, there were 242 detainees, all of them adversaries in the "War on Terror."

Despite his executive order, the detention camp remained open when Obama left the White House in 2017, as it does to this day. The question of why he did not succeed in closing the camp has been the subject of extensive debate.[314]

Some, including 2020 presidential hopeful Joe Biden, have blamed Congress for the delay, while many others placed responsibility at the feet of Obama. Congress did indeed take a number of steps to prevent closure of the camp, including a 54–41 Senate vote in 2012 to bar Guantánamo prisoners from being brought to the U.S. Yet many voices declared that Obama lacked the requisite will. For example, ACLU attorney Zachary Katznelson stated at the time that, "President Obama has enough control and power that he can get these men out today if he has the political will to do so."[315]

For whatever reason, Obama did not succeed in keeping his campaign promise to shut down the prison. There were forty-one inmates left when he handed over the reins of power to Donald

314 https://www.newyorker.com/magazine/2016/08/01/why-obama-has-failed-to-close-guantanamo
315 https://abcnews.go.com/Politics/OTUS/guantanamo-bay-open-promises/story?id=16698768

Trump. During a 2019 Democratic presidential primary debate, Biden railed against Gitmo, calling it an "advertisement for creating terror."[316]

316   https://pjmedia.com/election/nicholas-ballasy/2019/12/20/biden-guantanamo-bay-prison-an-advertisement-for-creating-terror-n43333

Armenian Genocide

Obama promised as a presidential candidate to recognize the massacres of an estimated 1.5 million Armenians between 1915 and 1922 by the Ottoman Empire as genocide. But, after his election, he did not do so, missing chances such as the one hundredth anniversary of the atrocities in 2015. Two top Obama aides later acknowledged the failure of the administration to officially recognize the genocide, admitting in 2018 that "It was a mistake."[317] Aram Suren Hamparian, executive director of the Armenian National Committee of America, said "President Obama should explain why he didn't honor his pledge. And I think he owes us an apology."

317 https://www.politico.com/story/2018/01/19/armenian-genocide-ben-rhodes-samantha-power-obama-349973

Two Terms, Two Wars

Before he took office in 2009, Obama pledged to end U.S. military interventions in Iraq and Afghanistan. Eight years later, he had the distinction of being the first two-term president to preside over American wars during every single day of his tenure.

PART V

JUSTICE

Gun Control

As a presidential candidate, Barack Obama advocated restrictions on the purchase of guns, including a robust background check for would-be buyers and a safety test for those specifically purchasing handguns.[318] A reauthorization of a ban on assault weapons and restrictions on gun show sales were also part of his proposals, which dovetailed with the Democratic platform.

Gun sales during the Obama presidency broke one record after another. The number of guns owned by private citizens climbed from 308 million units to more than 400 million by the time he left office.[319] This proliferation of firearms led the president to proclaim gun control as his "greatest frustration."[320]

Indeed, Obama actually expanded gun owners' rights. In 2009 and 2010, he signed into existence two laws dealing with guns. One reversed a measure instituted in the aftermath of 9/11 that barred Amtrak passengers from holding guns in checked bags, while the other allowed licensed gun owners to carry loaded firearms into the Grand Canyon and other national parks.[321] In 2011, Obama actually boasted that his administration "has not curtailed the rights of gun owners—it has expanded them, including allowing people to carry their guns in national parks and wildlife refuges."[322]

Moreover, Obama failed to eliminate a loophole he had pledged to abolish which lets certain individuals buy guns without a background check.[323] Nor could he get his own proposal that would have banned

318   https://edition.cnn.com/ELECTION/2008/issues/issues.gun.html
319   https://www.thetruthaboutguns.com/president-obamas-biggest-failure-gun-control/
320   https://www.bbc.co.uk/news/av/world-us-canada-33629023
321   https://www.businessinsider.com/gun-laws-obama-has-signed-2012-12?r=US&IR=T
322   https://www.thoughtco.com/obama-gun-laws-passed-by-congress-3367595
323   https://www.huffingtonpost.co.uk/entry/obama-gun-control-_n_5404854

firearms sales to anyone on a terrorist watch list passed, an eminently reasonable proposal if ever there were one.

The Brady Campaign to Prevent Gun Violence gave Obama an 'F' for his first year in office.[324] By the end of his second term, his record on gun control was widely regarded as weak. Perhaps it would have been advisable for him to remind the public that despite guns being more prevalent than ever, the number of U.S. homicides was at a fifty-year low.

Yet, however much Obama may have ignored this profound decline in violence inflicted by one individual on another, when it came to condemning gun violence in general, he was at his loquacious best. He unsparingly blamed the gun lobby, specifically the National Rifle Association, for preventing him from having any measures passed by Congress.

Obama did initiate a substantial number of executive actions "to reduce gun violence," including calling for mandatory criminal background checks on anyone buying a gun anywhere.[325] Executive actions, however, do not have the force of law of executive orders. They are explicitly non-binding.

A last-minute executive action put in place by Obama's administration was rescinded by his successor in 2017.[326] It mandated that the Social Security Administration report all disability-benefit recipients with mental illness classifications to the FBI's background check system. Donald Trump vowed during the 2016 presidential campaign to unsign this and other "terrible executive orders" implemented by Obama regarding guns as soon as he was in office.[327]

324 https://www.npr.org/sections/thetwo-way/2010/01/brady_campaign_gives_obama_an.html

325 https://obamawhitehouse.archives.gov/the-press-office/2016/01/04/fact-sheet-new-executive-actions-reduce-gun-violence-and-make-our

326 https://www.nbcnews.com/news/us-news/trump-signs-bill-revoking-obama-era-gun-checks-people-mental-n727221

327 https://www.youtube.com/watch?v=QyQD8M9yksI; https://www.politifact.com/truth-o-meter/promises/trumpometer/promise/1438/reverse-barack-obamas-2016-gun-executive-order/

Police Militarization

The 1994 Crime Bill, sponsored by Senator Joe Biden, initiated President Clinton's Community Oriented Policing Services (COPS), which provided federal grants to local police departments.[328] Although the program was largely phased out by the Bush administration, Obama and his newly minted running mate, Biden, promised during the 2008 presidential campaign to breathe new life into it. This was despite a 2005 Government Accountability Office report showing that between 1993 and 2000, COPS funds had contributed to a mere 1.3 percent decline in the overall crime rate and a 2.5 percent decline in the violent crime rate from the 1993 levels, at a cost of $7.6 billion.[329] A 2007 article published in the journal *Criminology* likewise found that "COPS spending had little to no effect on crime."[330]

Yet the effects of the COPS program were keenly felt in other ways. A 2001 investigation by the *Capital Times*, for example, found that COPS grants had contributed to an "explosion" of SWAT teams throughout Wisconsin, mainly in rural towns and most commonly used to serve drug warrants and make drug arrests.[331]

On the road to the White House, both Obama and Biden also strongly supported the Byrne Justice Assistance Grant (JAG) program, which was used to fund regional anti-drug task forces across the country. The program was not without its critics. In a June 2008 letter to House Judiciary leadership, the ACLU wrote that the Byrne program was "perpetuating racial disparities, police corruption, over-incarceration and civil rights abuses," and urged that it be discontinued unless

---

328 https://gen.medium.com/how-a-biden-backed-community-policing-bill-wound-up-militarizing-cops-81508eeb14a7
329 https://www.gao.gov/new.items/d06104.pdf
330 https://onlinelibrary.wiley.com/doi/abs/10.1111/j.1745-9125.2007.00075.x
331 https://madison.com/ct/news/local/writers/steven_elbow/hooked-on-swat/article_f1bc13e6-b29b-5ab0-a7cf-ba46b1b3860c.html

it were reformed.[332] Wrote *Slate* at the time: "Although Byrne has not failed to achieve its stated goal (reducing the availability of illicit drugs), it has made drug policing more aggressive and militaristic and less accountable. And by prioritizing raw arrest statistics, the program tends to focus police efforts on low-level offenders instead of major distributors."[333]

Yet, presidential candidate Obama promised during a September 2008 speech in Florida to restore full funding to Byrne, saying it "has been critical to creating the anti-gang and anti-drug task forces our communities need."[334]

In May 2015, President Obama delivered an ostensibly soothing message to the nation, following a series of news reports on police killings of unarmed Black men and the protest movement that had arisen as a result. Speaking in Camden, New Jersey, he announced that the federal government would no longer provide heavy military equipment like tanks and grenade launchers to local cops. The announcement came several months after images had shown police in helmets, goggles, and gas masks threatening protestors in Ferguson, Missouri with armored vehicles and assault rifles.

"We've seen how militarized gear can sometimes give people a feeling like there's an occupying force, as opposed to a force that's part of the community that's protecting them and serving them," Obama said.[335] "It can alienate and intimidate local residents, and send the wrong message. So we're going to prohibit some equipment made for the battlefield that is not appropriate for local police departments."

---

332 https://www.aclu.org/letter/aclu-coalition-letter-house-judiciary-leadership-urging-them-not-reauthorize-byrne-justice?redirect=cpredirect/35700

333 https://slate.com/news-and-politics/2008/10/obama-s-bad-criminal-justice-ideas.html

334 https://www.huffingtonpost.co.uk/entry/obama-police-militarization_n_3566478

335 https://www.nbcnews.com/news/us-news/u-s-cracking-down-militarization-local-police-n360381

Professor Peter Kraska of the School of Justice Studies at Eastern Kentucky University, decried the announcement as a publicity stunt. "All you had to do was barely scratch under the surface—and it's nothing more than symbolic politics," he told the *Guardian*.[336]

At issue was the 1033 program through which the Department of Defense (DoD) transfers surplus military equipment to local and state law enforcement nationwide. Of the seven prohibited equipment items listed by the White House, six had not been distributed to local law enforcement by the Pentagon for years, DoD spokesman Mark Wright also told the *Guardian*, explaining: "the only one that we were still issuing at this time were the bayonets."[337] Missing from the list were: modified M-16 assault rifles, Humvees, helicopters, night-vision goggles, mine-resistant ambush-protected vehicles (MRAPs), BearCat vehicles, military-style helmets, shin guards, and shields.

In addition, a 2016 investigation by *In These Times* found that "in practice, the president's much-ballyhooed reforms to the 1033 program have done little to stem the flow of battlefield gear to cops."[338] According to the investigation, the total value of equipment distributed through the program actually increased in the year following the ban. As of fiscal year 2016, the DoD had transferred $494 million worth of gear to local police departments, up from $418 million the previous fiscal year, *In These Times* learned.

336 https://www.theguardian.com/us-news/2015/may/22/obama-ban-police-military-gear-falls-short

337 https://www.theguardian.com/us-news/2015/may/22/obama-ban-police-military-gear-falls-short

338 https://inthesetimes.com/features/obama_police_miltary_equipment_ban.html

Military Tribunals

A year after pronouncing George W. Bush's military tribunal system "an enormous failure," President Obama revived it by signing into law the Military Commissions Act of 2009.[339] Although Obama had suspended the tribunals within hours of taking office, ordering a review of the military commission system, he ultimately kept them in place. Officials in his administration said the tribunals would be made fairer by limiting the use of hearsay and banning evidence gained from cruel treatment, including "waterboarding."[340]

Nonetheless, Obama was widely condemned by human rights organizations because the tribunal process bars defendants from rights they would be afforded in a civilian courtroom. "It's disappointing that Obama is seeking to revive rather than end this failed experiment," said Jonathan Hafetz of the American Civil Liberties Union.[341] "There's no detainee at Guantánamo who cannot be tried and shouldn't be tried in the regular federal courts system."

The first military tribunal to follow under Obama was the 2010 war crimes trial of Omar Khadr, who was arrested in Afghanistan in 2002 for crimes he had allegedly committed as a child. Khadr was fifteen when he allegedly threw a grenade that killed a U.S. soldier. "Since World War II, no child has been prosecuted for war crimes," Radhika Coomaraswamy, Secretary-General Ban Ki-moon's Special Representative for Children and Armed Conflict, said in a statement.[342] Coomaraswamy noted, as well, that the statute of the International Criminal Court was clear that no one under the age of eighteen should be tried for war crimes.

---

339 https://www.nytimes.com/2009/05/15/us/politics/15gitmo.html
340 https://www.theguardian.com/world/2009/may/15/barack-obama-revives-guantanamo-tribunals
341 https://www.theguardian.com/world/2009/may/15/barack-obama-revives-guantanamo-tribunals
342 https://news.un.org/en/story/2010/08/347282

In 2011, Obama's attorney general, Eric Holder, announced that Khalid Shaikh Mohammed (KSM) would also be prosecuted for war crimes before a military tribunal. "It's probably fair to say, as some newspapers have noted, that the idea of bringing KSM to New York City to be tried in civilian court for the 9/11 atrocity was Holder's 'signature' decision since becoming attorney general—and that that idea is now dead," wrote Tim Lynch in an article published by the Cato Institute.[343] "However, Obama and Holder conceded a place for tribunals more than a year ago and they could never really offer a good explanation as to why some persons would go to civilian court and why others would go before tribunals. Like Bush, Cheney, and Rumsfeld, Obama and his people would just sorta decide case-by-case."

The proper legal authority of the military tribunal system remains under question. In 2016, the U.S. Court of Appeals for the District of Columbia Circuit, the nation's second highest court, sided with the government in upholding a conspiracy conviction in the case of Guantánamo Bay detainee Ali Hamza Ahmad Suliman al-Bahlul.[344] The Yemeni citizen was sentenced to life in prison on November 3, 2008, after a jury in a military commissions trial found him guilty of terrorism charges. He was accused of being Osama bin Laden's "media secretary" and of making al-Qaeda recruitment videos, as well as video wills for two of the 9/11 hijackers.

In a six-to-three ruling on October 20, 2016, the appeals court upheld al-Bahlul's conviction for conspiracy to commit war crimes.[345] At issue was whether the Constitution allows Congress to make conspiracy to commit war crimes an offense triable by military commissions, despite the fact that the charge of conspiracy is considered a crime under domestic law but is not a war crime recognized by international

---

343   https://www.cato.org/blog/obama-military-tribunals
344   https://www.hrw.org/news/2013/03/05/ali-hamza-ahmad-suliman-al-bahlul
345   http://www.andyworthington.co.uk/2016/10/29/in-contentious-split-decision-appeals-court-upholds-guantanamo-prisoner-ali-hamza-al-bahluls-conspiracy-conviction/

law. Four of the six judges in the majority, including Brett Kavanaugh, argued that Congress had the constitutional power to authorize conspiracy charges in the military commission. The other two judges in the majority voted to uphold the decision for different legal reasons.

"The divided ruling," the *New York Times*' Charlie Savage wrote at the time, "left unresolved a broader legal question that could help determine whether the tribunals system takes root as a permanent alternative to civilian court for prosecuting terrorism suspects, or fades away after the handful of current cases comes to an end."[346] In October 2017, the U.S. Supreme Court refused to hear an appeal from the decision.[347] As of October 2020, Al-Bahlul remained in detention at Guantánamo.

346 https://www.nytimes.com/2016/10/21/us/guantanamo-detainees-conspiracy-conviction-upheld-but-legal-issue-lingers.html
347 https://www.miamiherald.com/news/nation-world/world/americas/guantanamo/article178042466.html

TSA

At a November 2010 NATO press conference in Lisbon, President Obama held his ground against criticism of his adoption of extra Transportation Security Administration (TSA) measures at American airports. He noted that body scans and pat-downs were vital elements in the fight against terrorism in the skies. In doing so, he referenced the so-called Underwear Bomber, Umar Farouk Abdulmutallab, who had boarded a 2009 Christmas flight from Amsterdam to Detroit with a bomb hidden in his underpants.

Abdulmutallab had failed to fully detonate the explosive, which metal detectors missed. Nevertheless, the would-be bomber's attempt was instrumental in pushing airports to adopt the new screening procedures, turning the 2010 holiday travel season into a cornucopia of complaints.

In Lisbon, Obama proclaimed that the TSA, "in consultation with our counterterrorism experts, have indicated to me that the procedures that they've been putting in place are the only ones right now that they consider to be effective against the kind of threat that we saw in the Christmas Day bombing."[348]

John Whitehead, president of the civil liberties-oriented Rutherford Institute, argued that the new rules promulgated under Obama were "forcing travelers to consent to a virtual strip search or allow an unknown officer to literally place his or her hands in your pants."[349]

But Obama was undeterred. "One of the most frustrating aspects of this fight against terrorism is that it has created a whole security

348 https://obamawhitehouse.archives.gov/the-press-office/2010/11/20/press-conference-president-after-nato-summit
349 https://edition.cnn.com/2010/TRAVEL/11/20/obama.tsa/index.html#:~:text=Critics%20have%20called%20the%20procedures,her%20hands%20in%20your%20pants.%22

apparatus around us that causes huge inconvenience for all of us," the president explained.[350]

What Obama did not touch on was the abysmal performance over the years of the TSA's weapons detections tests. In 2015, for instance, a leaked Department of Homeland Security report showed that auditors were able to get fake weapons and explosives past security screeners 95 percent of the time in seventy covert tests.[351]

More than 750 million travelers pass through TSA portals each year, yet the TSA is not known to have caught a single terrorist.[352]

At the Lisbon press conference, Obama also did not explain the seemingly arbitrary process behind the choice of locations for these airport security zone cordons. By way of example, the 2016 terror attack at Brussels Airport took place in an area where a large group of people were standing in line to check in.[353] This demonstrated the obvious—that passengers in such congested lines are sitting ducks.

Many crowded places at airports, such as restaurants and shops outside of secured zones, are similarly compromised in terms of adequate security. What about TSA waiting lines or curbside drop-offs? What about malls, high school football games, or movie theaters? Why the fixation on airplanes?

From September 12, 2001 to December 31, 2016, 225 people were killed in the United States in attacks by violent extremists.[354] Of these, three were killed at an American airport, with an additional five slain in 2017. Compare this with the 800,000 Americans who, as of 2017,

---

350 https://obamawhitehouse.archives.gov/the-press-office/2010/11/20/press-conference-president-after-nato-summit

351 https://www.nbcnews.com/news/us-news/investigation-breaches-us-airports-allowed-weapons-through-n367851

352 https://www.tsa.gov/sites/default/files/resources/tsabythenumbers_factsheet.pdf

353 https://www.bbc.co.uk/news/world-europe-35869985

354 https://www.politifact.com/article/2017/aug/16/look-data-domestic-terrorism-and-whos-behind-it/

die from cardiovascular causes every year.[355] The fifteen-year figure for victims of extremist attacks in the United States is approximately twice the number of Americans who die of heart disease in one hour.

Public funding for cardiovascular disease research totals $2 billion a year, or about $2,500 per victim of a fatality.[356] By a conservative estimation, the U.S. spent approximately ninety-three times as much annually from fiscal years 2002 to 2017 on counterterrorism ($186 billion), or about $827 million per fatality.[357]

---

355   https://www.acc.org/latest-in-cardiology/ten-points-to-remember/2017/
02/09/14/58/heart-disease-and-stroke-statistics-2017
356   https://report.nih.gov/categorical_spending.aspx
357   https://www.defensenews.com/pentagon/2018/05/16/heres-how-much-the-us-has-spent-fighting-terrorism-since-911/

Whistleblowers

As a presidential candidate, Obama pledged in 2008 to bolster whistleblower laws for federal workers by expediting the review process for claims and granting whistleblowers full access to jury trials and due process.[358] He claimed, "Often the best source of information about waste, fraud, and abuse in government is an existing government employee committed to public integrity and willing to speak out. Such acts of courage and patriotism, which can sometimes save lives and often save taxpayer dollars, should be encouraged rather than stifled."[359]

In 2012, responding to an accusation that his White House had purposely leaked classified information to appear tough on national security, Obama had clearly changed his tune: "Since I've been in office, my attitude has been zero tolerance for these kinds of leaks and speculation. Now we have mechanisms in place where, if we can root out folks who have leaked, they will suffer consequences. In some cases, it's criminal. These are criminal acts when they release information like this. And we will conduct thorough investigations, as we have in the past."[360]

The same year, Obama signed both an executive order and a law improving whistleblower protection rights. More victims could now claim whistleblower status and, for the first time, whistleblowers could sue for damages as victims of reprisal. The law, however, did not give whistleblowers access to jury trials. It also left out protections for whistleblowers in the intelligence community, most notably former NSA contractor Edward Snowden.

---

358 https://www.politifact.com/truth-o-meter/promises/obameter/promise/426/increase-protections-for-whistleblowers/
359 https://www.huffingtonpost.co.uk/entry/obama-whistleblower-website_n_3658815?ri18n=true
360 https://www.theguardian.com/world/2012/jun/08/obama-denies-leaks-national-security

Obama followed up with Presidential Policy Directive 19, an executive order expanding whistleblower protections to national security and intelligence employees. The order, however, aimed to keep whistleblower complaints internal rather than in the media. If necessary, a whistleblower could take a complaint to Congress.

During the Obama administration, the Department of Justice brought charges under the Espionage Act against eight people accused of leaking to the media: Thomas Drake, Shamai Leibowitz, Stephen Kim, Chelsea Manning, Donald Sachtleben, Jeffrey Sterling, John Kiriakou, and Edward Snowden.[361] Two other high-ranking Obama officials, General David Petraeus and General James Cartwright, were also prosecuted as part of leak investigations.[362] They both ultimately pled to lesser charges and were never indicted under the Espionage Act. Cartwright was also later pardoned. Including their cases, the total number of leak case prosecutions under the Obama administration was ten.

"By my count, the Obama administration has secured 526 months of prison time for national security leakers, versus only 24 months total jail time for everyone else since the American Revolution," wrote Gabe Rottman, legislative counsel with the ACLU.[363]

In 2017, Obama commuted Manning's thirty-five-year sentence for making disclosures to WikiLeaks. He stated in a press conference that the sentence was "very disproportionate relative to what other leakers have received" and that "it makes sense to commute—and not pardon—her sentence."[364]

---

361 https://slate.com/news-and-politics/2013/06/edward-snowden-is-eighth-person-obama-has-pursued-under-espionage-act.html
362 https://freedom.press/news/obama-used-espionage-act-put-record-number-reporters-sources-jail-and-trump-could-be-even-worse/
363 https://www.aclu.org/blog/free-speech/employee-speech-and-whistleblowers/leak-prosecutions-obama-takes-it-11-or-should-we
364 https://www.theguardian.com/us-news/2017/jan/18/barack-obama-final-press-conference-chelsea-manning

TIME called the Manning commutation a "good deed" that, "should not obliterate his otherwise awful legacy on whistleblowers and leakers."[365] Noted *TIME* in 2017:

> "Manning's disclosures to WikiLeaks in 2010 were voluminous, but she had no chance to argue at her trial that they were in the public interest or exposed wrongdoing, and the government never had to prove that the leaks did serious harm. (It still hasn't.) That's because the benefit/harm question is irrelevant to the antiquated 1917 Espionage Act, which was designed to punish people who leaked government secrets to a foreign government, not to the media."

---

365 https://time.com/4638617/chelsea-manning-commutation-obama-whistleblower-legacy/

Torture

Prior to commuting Chelsea Manning's thirty-five-year sentence for leaking classified information, President Obama spoke in defense of her treatment while in detention—treatment that had been widely derided as cruel and inhuman. The former Bradley Manning had been in military custody for ten months when Obama addressed the issue in a March 2011 White House press conference: "With respect to Private Manning, I have actually asked the Pentagon whether or not the procedures that have been taken in terms of his confinement are appropriate and are meeting our basic standards. They assure me that they are."[366]

A week before the press conference, the *New York Times* reported that brig officials were stripping Manning of all his clothing and forcing him to remain naked.[367] In January 2011, Amnesty International called on the U.S. Government to end the "unnecessarily harsh and punitive" pre-trial detention conditions under which the Army whistleblower was being held in Quantico, Va.[368] The conditions included being held for twenty-three hours a day in a sparsely furnished solitary cell and being deprived of a pillow, sheets, and personal possessions.

After a public outcry that included a letter of protest signed by more than 250 leading U.S. legal scholars who questioned Obama's standards of decency in handling the case, Manning was moved in April 2011 to a windowed cell at Fort Leavenworth, Kansas.

Juan Méndez, the UN special rapporteur on torture, formally concluded in February 2012 that the U.S. government was, at minimum, guilty of cruel, inhuman, and degrading treatment during Manning's total eleven-month detention in Quantico.[369] Méndez was not able to reach a definitive conclusion on whether Manning had been

---

366 https://www.nytimes.com/2011/03/12/us/12manning.html
367 https://www.nytimes.com/2011/03/04/us/04manning.html
368 https://www.amnestyusa.org/the-bradley-manning-trials/
369 https://www.ohchr.org/Documents/HRBodies/HRCouncil/RegularSession/Session19/A_HRC_19_61_Add.4_EFSonly.pdf

tortured because he was consistently denied permission by the U.S. Military to interview the prisoner under acceptable (unmonitored) circumstances.[370]

As a presidential candidate in 2007, Obama had called torture "wrong-headed, as well as immoral."[371] A few weeks into office, he signed an executive order to ban enhanced interrogation techniques, including waterboarding, and made the pronouncement that "the United States of America does not torture."[372]

Nonetheless, Obama went on to appoint John Brennan, a key figure in crafting and carrying out U.S. torture policy, as his director of the CIA from 2013 to 2017.[373] Under the Obama administration, the U.S. also reportedly:

- Authorized the CIA to continue renditions, secret abductions, and transfers of prisoners to countries that cooperated with the United States, despite allegations that prisoners were tortured.[374]

- Blocked victims of such "extraordinary renditions" from suing the Government.[375]

- Allegedly abused detainees at a super-secret prison on the periphery of Bagram Air Base in Afghanistan.[376]

- Trained Afghan security forces who, according to a UN report, may have engaged in "a compelling pattern and practice of

370 https://www.theguardian.com/world/2012/mar/12/bradley-manning-cruel-inhuman-treatment-un

371 https://www.nytimes.com/2007/10/04/us/politics/04obama-text.html

372 https://obamawhitehouse.archives.gov/the-press-office/ensuring-lawful-interrogations; https://www.reuters.com/article/us-obama-torture-sb/america-does-not-torture-obama-tells-congress-idUSTRE51O0RY20090225

373 https://www.huffingtonpost.co.uk/entry/john-brennan-torture-tain_n_145517?ri18n=true

374 https://www.latimes.com/archives/la-xpm-2009-feb-01-na-rendition1-story.html

375 https://www.aclu.org/press-releases/obama-administration-seeks-keep-torture-victims-having-day-court?redirect=cpredirect/39843

376 http://news.bbc.co.uk/1/hi/8621973.stm

systematic torture and ill-treatment" in interrogations at intelligence agency detention centers, including the notorious Department 124. Practices recounted by former detainees included being hung by the wrists from chains attached to walls or ceilings, being beaten with rubber hoses and electric cables, having their genitals twisted and wrenched, receiving electric shocks, and being denied access to doctors for their injuries.[377]

- Oversaw a worsening of prisoner abuse at Guantánamo Bay, according to a lawyer who represented detainees.[378]

377 https://unama.unmissions.org/sites/default/files/october10_2011_unama_detention_full-report_eng.pdf
378 https://www.reuters.com/article/us-guantanamo-abuse-lawyer-exclusive/exclusive-lawyer-says-guantanamo-abuse-worse-since-obama-idUSTRE51O3TB20090225?sp=true

Assassination of U.S. Citizens

The American Civil Liberties Union and the Center for Constitutional Rights sued the Obama administration in 2012, charging that the U.S. government's killings of three U.S. citizens the previous year had "violated the Constitution's fundamental guarantee against the deprivation of life without due process of law."[379] Anwar al-Aulaqi and Samir Khan were killed in a drone strike in Yemen, and then, two weeks later, in circumstances that were never explained, al-Aulaqi's sixteen-year-old American son, Abdulrahman, was killed in a separate drone strike in Yemen.[380]

The three were targeted as part of an Obama hit list that operated outside the context of armed conflict. "The program is based on vague legal standards, a closed executive decision-making process, and evidence never presented to the courts, even after the killing," the ACLU said in a statement.[381] According to the legal complaint, the killings violated international law, as well as the Fifth Amendment right to due process, the Fourth Amendment prohibition on unreasonable seizures, and, in the case of Anwar Al-Aulaqi, the ban on extrajudicial death warrants imposed by the Constitution's Bill of Attainder Clause.

Despite a lawsuit by the *New York Times*, the Obama administration refused to disclose the legal memoranda prepared by the president's lawyers that set forth their legal rationale for the president's assassination power.[382]

---

379 https://www.aclu.org/cases/al-aulaqi-v-panetta-constitutional-challenge-killing-three-us-citizens

380 https://www.amnestyusa.org/is-it-legal-for-the-u-s-to-kill-a-16-year-old-u-s-citizen-with-a-drone/

381 https://www.aclu.org/cases/al-aulaqi-v-panetta-constitutional-challenge-killing-three-us-citizens

382 https://thehill.com/policy/defense/201197-new-york-times-sues-justice-department-over-targeted-killing-memo; https://uk.reuters.com/article/us-newyorktimes-drone-lawsuit/ny-times-loses-bid-to-uncover-details-on-drone-strikes-idUSBRE90100V20130102

"In sum, Obama not only claims he has the power to order U.S. citizens killed with no transparency, but that even the documents explaining the legal rationale for this power are to be concealed," wrote Glenn Greenwald in the *Guardian*.[383] He explained:

"What has made these actions all the more radical is the absolute secrecy with which Obama has draped all of this. Not only is the entire process carried out solely within the Executive branch with no checks or oversight of any kind—but there is zero transparency and zero accountability. The president's underlings compile their proposed lists of who should be executed, and the president—at a charming weekly event dubbed by White House aides as 'Terror Tuesday'—then chooses from 'baseball cards' and decrees in total secrecy who should die. The power of accuser, prosecutor, judge, jury, and executioner are all consolidated in this one man, and those powers are exercised in the dark."

383 https://www.theguardian.com/commentisfree/2013/feb/05/obama-kill-list-doj-memo

NDAA and Habeas Corpus

The Patriot Act, enacted in the wake of 9/11, allowed the U.S. government to spy on Americans in order to identify terrorists. Under this Act, the government would not be required to show evidence that subjects of search orders were an "agent of foreign power," nor even a reasonable suspicion that records collected on subjects were related to criminal activity.[384] The Act also allowed for the indefinite detention of non-U.S. citizens.

Years later, H.R. 1540, the National Defense Authorization Act for fiscal year 2012, included a provision allowing for U.S. citizens suspected of terrorist activity to be detained for indefinite periods as well. This provision, section 1021 of the NDAA, was widely condemned as unconstitutional. Nonetheless, Obama signed it, a move Human Rights Watch called "a historic tragedy for rights."[385]

The bill also required that the U.S. military take custody of certain terrorism suspects, even inside the United States, cases that had up until then been adjudicated by federal, state, and local law enforcement authorities. "The law replaces an effective system of civilian-court prosecution with a system that has generated the kind of global outrage that would delight recruiters of terrorists," Kenneth Roth, HWR's executive director, said in a statement.[386]

A *Washington Post* opinion piece responded to Obama's action by posing the question, "At what point does the reduction of individual rights in our country change how we define ourselves?"[387] The author,

---

384 https://www.aclu.org/other/surveillance-under-usapatriot-act

385 https://www.hrw.org/news/2011/12/14/us-refusal-veto-detainee-bill-historic-tragedy-rights

386 https://www.hrw.org/news/2011/12/14/us-refusal-veto-detainee-bill-historic-tragedy-rights

387 https://www.washingtonpost.com/opinions/is-the-united-states-still-the-land-of-the-free/2012/01/04/gIQAvcD1wP_story.html

Jonathan Turley, a law professor at George Washington University, explained that,

> "Under the law signed last month, terrorism suspects are to be held by the military; the president also has the authority to indefinitely detain citizens accused of terrorism. While the administration claims that this provision only codified existing law, experts widely contest this view, and the administration has opposed efforts to challenge such authority in federal courts. The government continues to claim the right to strip citizens of legal protections based on its sole discretion."

Further objections to the bill followed claims by Senator Carl Levin (D-MI) that the White House had specifically demanded that provisions excluding U.S. citizens on U.S. soil from indefinite military detention be removed from the bill.

In a White House signing statement accompanying H.R. 1540, Obama noted that he had signed it despite "having serious reservations" over certain provisions:

> "Over the last several years, my Administration has developed an effective, sustainable framework for the detention, interrogation and trial of suspected terrorists that allows us to maximize both our ability to collect intelligence and to incapacitate dangerous individuals in rapidly developing situations, and the results we have achieved are undeniable. Our success against al-Qa'ida and its affiliates and adherents has derived in significant measure from providing our counterterrorism professionals with the clarity and flexibility they need to adapt to changing circumstances and to utilize whichever authorities best protect the American people, and our accomplishments have respected the values that make our country an example for the world. Against that record of success, some in Congress continue to insist upon restricting the options available to our counterterrorism professionals and interfering with the very operations that have kept us safe. My Administration has consistently opposed such measures."[388]

388 https://obamawhitehouse.archives.gov/the-press-office/2011/12/31/statement-president-hr-1540

In other words, Obama's reservations were due not to his distaste for indefinitely detaining people without trial, but to restrictions the bill placed on the president's sole power to do so.

The fact that the indefinite detention of U.S. citizens for suspected terrorist activity remained on the books when Obama left office is troubling. It is an insouciant snub directed at the First, Fourth, Fifth, and Sixth Amendments of the Bill of Rights.

Deportation

During the first three fiscal years of the Obama administration, the U.S. Immigration and Customs Enforcement (ICE) removed 1.18 million people from the U.S.[389] In 2012 alone, the administration deported 409,849 people. The number of removals during the first three fiscal years of the Trump administration was around 800,000, a difference of about 400,000.

"Felons, not families. Criminals, not children. Gang members, not a mom who's working hard to provide for her kids. We'll prioritize, just like law enforcement does every day," Obama said when announcing his November 2014 executive action on immigration.[390] Despite Obama's professed focus on deporting criminals, of the 3 million people removed from the U.S. in total under his administration, 1.7 million of them had no criminal record.[391]

Donald Trump promised to "immediately" deport 2 to 3 million undocumented immigrants upon taking office and, on January 25, 2017, signed two executive orders promising wide-ranging expansions of the enforcement system, including prioritizing the removal not only of noncitizens with criminal records, but also those deemed to pose a risk to national security and those who abuse public benefits.[392] Yet, despite Trump's strong anti-migrant stance, the most deportations

389 https://thehill.com/latino/470900-deportations-lower-under-trump-than-obama-report

390 https://obamawhitehouse.archives.gov/the-press-office/2014/11/20/remarks-president-address-nation-immigration

391 https://abcnews.go.com/Politics/wireStory/time-biden-calls-obama-deportations-big-mistake-69010125

392 https://www.independent.co.uk/news/world/americas/donald-trump-deport-immigrants-immediately-when-mexico-wall-a7415116.html; https://www.whitehouse.gov/presidential-actions/executive-order-border-security-immigration-enforcement-improvements/; https://www.whitehouse.gov/presidential-actions/executive-order-enhancing-public-safety-interior-united-states/

carried out by ICE in a single fiscal year under his administration (as of October 2020) were 267,258 in 2019, as compared to Obama's high of 409,849 in 2012.[393]

393 https://www.axios.com/immigration-ice-deportation-trump-obama-a72a0a44-540d-46bc-a671-cd65cf72f4b1.html; https://www.ice.gov/sites/default/files/documents/Document/2019/eroReportFY2019.pdf

War on Drugs

During a stump speech at Howard University before the 2008 presidential election, Obama promised that if elected, he would do one better than the current president in the area of drug reform:

> "Someone once said that '… long minimum sentences for first-time users may not be the best way to occupy jail space and/or heal people from their disease.' That someone was George W. Bush—six years ago. I don't say this very often, but I agree with the President. The difference is, he hasn't done anything about it. When I'm President, I will. We will review these sentences to see where we can be smarter on crime and reduce the blind and counterproductive warehousing of non-violent offenders."[394]

In 2013, Obama reduced the sentences of eight prisoners who were serving long federal prison terms under pre-2010 laws for crack-cocaine sentencing.[395] Six of them were in for life. He also pardoned thirteen other mostly minor offenders. The eight who received commutations had been serving racially discriminatory sentences for crack cocaine, under a disparity that issued sentences one hundred times harsher for crack cocaine, associated with African Americans, than for powder cocaine, associated with whites.

Perversely, the law that created the sentencing disparity, the Anti-Drug Abuse Act of 1986, was sponsored and partly written by Obama's own vice president, former senator Joe Biden.[396] This was not an anomaly. With Senator Strom Thurmond, Biden also spearheaded the 1984 Comprehensive Control Act, which expanded federal drug trafficking

---

394 https://web.archive.org/web/20101227120246/http://www.barackobama.com/2007/09/28/remarks_of_senator_barack_obam_26.php

395 https://thinkprogress.org/obama-uses-pardon-power-to-release-prisoners-sentenced-under-draconian-drug-laws-2d6a36af4e2c/

396 https://www.washingtonpost.com/politics/how-an-early-biden-crime-bill-created-the-sentencing-disparity-for-crack-and-cocaine-trafficking/2019/07/28/5cbb4c98-9dcf-11e9-85d6-5211733f92c7_story.html

penalties. He co-sponsored the Anti-Drug Abuse Act of 1988, which strengthened prison sentences for drug possession, enhanced penalties for transporting drugs, and established the Office of National Drug Control Policy to coordinate and lead federal anti-drug efforts. Biden bragged in 1991 that, due to laws passed under his and Thurmond's leadership, a person caught with a piece of crack cocaine "no bigger than [a] quarter" would receive a mandatory five-year sentence, with no parole.[397]

Biden also partly wrote the 1994 Crime Bill (the Violent Crime Control and Law Enforcement Act), which provided $9.7 billion in funding for prisons and additional funding to hire one hundred thousand new police officers, contributing to the growth of the U.S. prison population from the 1990s through the 2000s. The Act also created sixty new death penalty offenses, gave incentive grants to build and expand correctional facilities to states that adopted "truth-in-sentencing" laws that scaled back parole, and effectively eliminated higher education for lower-income prison inmates.[398]

In 2010, in a move backed by a conciliatory Biden, Congress reduced the crack-cocaine sentencing disparity to eighteen-to-one when it passed the Fair Sentencing Act, but because the law was not retroactive, those sentenced to mandatory minimum prison terms before 2010 remained behind bars.

Before issuing his 2013 sentencing reductions, Obama had commuted only one sentence out of 8,700 commutation applications, according to Families Against Mandatory Minimums.[399] During his final weeks in the White House, however, he more than doubled the

397 https://www.c-span.org/video/?c4802783/user-clip-joe-biden-praises-crack-possession-laws

398 https://www.vox.com/policy-and-politics/2019/6/20/18677998/joe-biden-1994-crime-bill-law-mass-incarceration; https://www.theatlantic.com/politics/archive/2019/11/how-biden-killed-educational-opportunity-prisons/601120/

399 https://thinkprogress.org/obama-uses-pardon-power-to-release-prisoners-sentenced-under-draconian-drug-laws-2d6a36af4e2c/

number of people he had pardoned up until then, bringing his total number of clemency recipients to 1,324.[400] Most of them were serving long prison sentences for relatively minor drug crimes. Obama was widely lauded for using his clemency powers more times than all the previous eleven presidents combined.

That characterization was misleading, according to the law professor who set up the first clemency legal clinic in the country and represented more than sixty petitioners. Mark Osler, a law professor at the University of St Thomas, noted that Obama held such a distinction only when discounting the clemency record of Gerald Ford. "In 1974, the Republican president granted clemency to 14,000 draft dodgers and deserters of the Vietnam war," wrote the *Guardian*. "That was a brave move, Osler contends, given that at the time 'draft dodgers were as popular as crack dealers are today.'"[401]

Osler told the *Guardian* that Ford's much higher clemency rate was achieved via a lean bipartisan operation that pushed petitions through minimal bureaucracy. By contrast, he said, the Obama clemency project was so cumbersome that any prisoner had to negotiate to have his or her petition granted, and that the vast majority of the more than 30,000 prisoners who petitioned the president were denied clemency. "For the 1,324 beneficiaries, this was an incredible act of grace," Osler said. "The restoration to society matters, not just to them but to their families and communities. The problem is, I feel like the person after the shipwreck in the lifeboat seeing all the other people in the water."

Before leaving the White House, Obama brought his total number of commutations to 1,715.[402]

---

400 https://obamawhitehouse.archives.gov/blog/2016/12/19/president-obama-grants-153-commutations-and-78-pardons-individuals-deserving-second

401 https://www.theguardian.com/us-news/2017/jan/12/obama-clemency-pardons-commutations-war-on-drugs

402 https://www.justice.gov/pardon/clemency-statistics#obama

Solitary Confinement

Addressing a committee of the UN General Assembly in 2011, Juan Méndez, the Special Rapporteur on Torture, called on all countries to ban solitary confinement as a punishment or extortion technique, except in very exceptional circumstances and for as short a time as possible.[403] He said the practice could amount to torture. Méndez, himself a torture survivor, said that solitary confinement in excess of fifteen days should be subject to an absolute prohibition. He cited scientific studies showing that lasting mental damage is caused after a few days of social isolation.

The UN's Mandela Rules, adopted in December 2015, dictate that solitary confinement (confinement of prisoners for twenty-two hours or more a day without meaningful human contact) should be used only in exceptional cases as a last resort, for as short a time as possible, subject to independent review and only pursuant to the authorization by a competent authority.[404] The rules state it should never be used with youth and those with mental or physical disability or illness, and never for more than fifteen days, which is considered prolonged solitary confinement.

President Obama announced in July 2015 that he had asked the attorney general to review "the overuse of solitary confinement across American prisons."[405] The following January, in an op-ed for the *Washington Post*, he announced an executive order banning almost all use of solitary confinement for juveniles in federal prisons, although

---

403 https://news.un.org/en/story/2011/10/392012-solitary-confinement-should-be-banned-most-cases-un-expert-says
404 https://undocs.org/A/RES/70/175
405 https://obamawhitehouse.archives.gov/the-press-office/2016/01/25/fact-sheet-department-justice-review-solitary-confinement

few juveniles are charged with federal crimes.[406] The federal action also laid out fifty "Guiding Principles" that included reducing the time a high-level first-time offender can be committed to solitary confinement from a maximum of 365 days to 60 days, and from 545 days to 90 days for subsequent offenses; diverting inmates with serious mental illness to alternative forms of housing; and limiting the use of 'punitive segregation.'"[407]

Obama expressed his hope that the executive order would "serve as a model for state and local corrections systems," where most prisoners, and the vast majority of juveniles, are housed—tens of thousands in solitary confinement.[408]

Late in 2016, in response to Obama's executive order, the Pepperdine Law Review published a comment titled, "Protecting America's Children: Why an Executive Order Banning Juvenile Solitary Confinement Is Not Enough."[409] It noted:

> "Possibly the most important section of Obama's op-ed was his appeal to Congress. The president wrote that he hoped Congress 'will send [him] legislation as soon as possible that makes our criminal justice system smarter, fairer, less expensive and more effective.' In this one sentence, the president acknowledged what decades of jurisprudence has set in stone as truth: the president's power is at its weakest when he or she is acting alone."

406 https://www.washingtonpost.com/opinions/barack-obama-why-we-must-rethink-solitary-confinement/2016/01/25/29a361f2-c384-11e5-8965-0607e0e265ce_story.html

407 https://obamawhitehouse.archives.gov/the-press-office/2016/01/25/fact-sheet-department-justice-review-solitary-confinement

408 https://www.washingtonpost.com/opinions/barack-obama-why-we-must-rethink-solitary-confinement/2016/01/25/29a361f2-c384-11e5-8965-0607e0e265ce_story.html

409 https://digitalcommons.pepperdine.edu/plr/vol44/iss1/4/

Further, the report argued, in order to ensure Obama's ban extended to subsequent generations of incarcerated people, Congress and the Supreme Court "must recognize juvenile solitary confinement as a violation of the Eighth Amendment's Cruel and Unusual Punishment Clause. For this reason, it is essential that Obama's executive order be considered just one step—albeit a very significant one—towards eradicating juvenile solitary confinement in the United States."

White-Collar Crime

A 2011 Department of Defense report to Congress, prepared at the request of Senator Bernie Sanders, showed extensive defense contracting fraud over the previous three years. Sanders said in a statement that the report "detailed how the Pentagon spent $270 billion from 2007 to 2009 on 91 contractors involved in civil fraud cases that resulted in judgments of more than $1 million. Another $682 million went to 30 contractors convicted of hard-core criminal fraud in the same three-year period. Billions more went to firms that had been suspended or debarred by the Pentagon for misusing taxpayer dollars."[410]

The report was a requirement of a Sanders provision in a defense spending bill that also directed the Obama DoD to recommend ways to punish fraudulent contractors. Yet the Pentagon made no such recommendations.

Wrote Neil Gordon, an investigator with the Project on Government Oversight: "The fact that the report doesn't recommend any significant changes to DoD policies or practices is [...] raising eyebrows. It touts the initiatives DoD is undertaking in order to 'improve awareness and safeguards' with regard to contract fraud. Otherwise, the Pentagon 'believes that existing remedies with respect to contractor wrongdoing are sufficient.'"[411]

Under a separate Sanders provision in another law signed by Obama, the Supplemental Appropriations Act of 2010, a government-wide federal contractor fraud database was to be made accessible to the public later that year. Unfortunately, this effort toward

---

410 https://www.sanders.senate.gov/newsroom/press-releases/release-pentagon-spent-billions-on-contractors-that-committed-fraud; https://www.thenation.com/article/archive/pentagon-fraud-papers-contractors-defrauded-dod-were-rewarded-285-billion-new-contracts/

411 https://pogoblog.typepad.com/pogo/2011/02/dog-bites-man-in-pentagon-contracting-fraud-report.html

increased transparency was limited by the condition that the public version of the database would not provide contractors' past performance reviews.[412]

By 2015, under Obama, prosecutions of federal white-collar crime were on track to reach a twenty-year low, according to a preliminary report from Transactional Records Access Clearinghouse (TRAC), a data gathering, data research, and data distribution organization at Syracuse University.[413] During the first nine months of fiscal year 2015, the number of white-collar crime prosecutions was 5,173. TRAC Reports projected that if the year's pace were to continue until the end of FY 2015, the total would reach only 6,897, a drop of about one-third (36.8 percent) from 1995, and a 12.3-percent drop from 2014. White-collar crimes include violations of laws that involve tax, securities, bankruptcy, health care, antitrust, and federal procurement.

"The decline in federal white collar crime prosecutions does not necessarily indicate there has been a decline in white collar crime," noted TRAC Reports. "Rather, it may reflect shifting enforcement policies by each of the administrations and the various agencies, the changing availabilities of essential staff and congressionally mandated alterations in the laws. Because such enforcement by state and local agencies for these crimes sometimes is erratic or nonexistent, the declining role of the federal government could be of great significance."

---

412 https://www.pogo.org/press/release/2011/obama-administration-plan-to-open-contractor-database-to-public-fails-to-provide-full-access-to-responsibility-histories/
413 https://trac.syr.edu/tracreports/crim/398/

Supreme Court Nominee Rejected

President Obama's successful nominations of Sonia Sotomayor and Elena Kagan to the U.S. Supreme Court left the liberals, with four seats, one vote short of a majority on the bench. The opportunity to fill a third Supreme Court vacancy following the 2016 death of arch-conservative Justice Antonin Scalia could have resulted in that majority.

After Scalia's demise, Obama nominated Merrick Garland, the chief judge of the United States Court of Appeals for the District of Columbia Circuit. But before Obama had even named Garland, Republicans in the Senate announced in February 2016 that they would not vote on any Supreme Court nomination, nor even hold a committee hearing on a nominee.[414] Seeking to justify their decision, Republicans pointed to a 1992 speech by Vice President Joe Biden, in which he said that in a presidential election year the Senate should "not consider holding hearings until after the election."[415] They argued that it should be up to the new president, with putatively years ahead on the job, to nominate the next justice.

This was historically unprecedented, as with every one of the 103 earlier Supreme Court vacancies, the sitting president was able to both nominate and appoint a replacement with the Senate's approval. This did not always happen on the first try, but in the end, it always transpired. In a March 2016 statement stressing Merrick's suitability for the position as "one of America's sharpest legal minds," Obama urged: "I simply ask Republicans in the Senate to give him a fair hearing, and then an up or down vote. If you don't, then it will not only be an abdication of the Senate's constitutional duty, it will

---

414   https://www.theguardian.com/law/2016/feb/23/obama-supreme-court-nominee-senate-hearing-vote
415   https://www.politifact.com/article/2016/mar/17/context-biden-rule-supreme-court-nominations/

indicate a process for nominating and confirming judges that is beyond repair."[416]

Despite furious attacks from Democrats and overwhelming public and academic pressure, Republicans remained steadfast in their refusal to consider Garland's nomination. In August, Senate Majority Leader Mitch McConnell boasted to supporters in Kentucky: "One of my proudest moments was when I looked Barack Obama in the eye and I said, 'Mr. President, you will not fill the Supreme Court vacancy.'"[417]

The Garland nomination expired on the last day of the 114th Congress, about a fortnight before the Trump inauguration.[418]

The Republican senators' refusal to vote on Garland broke a venerable tradition of nominees being approved or rejected on their own merits, and not on the basis of the party affiliation of the nominating president. This prevented a liberal majority from materializing at the time, and with Donald Trump's ascension to the presidency, hopes for a liberal majority were scotched for a seemingly long while.

This legislative roadblock put up by the Republicans prevented Garland from taking his place as the tiebreaker on a court deadlocked 4-4 between liberals on one hand and conservatives, along with a lone moderate, on the other.

Garland's position as the fifth liberal out of nine justices would have indeed dramatically altered the court's ideological landscape, transitioning it from a conservative hue to a much more progressive shade.[419]

---

416   https://obamawhitehouse.archives.gov/the-press-office/2016/03/16/remarks-president-announcing-judge-merrick-garland-his-nominee-supreme

417   https://www.cbsnews.com/news/mitch-mcconnell-supreme-court-vacancy-election-year-senate/

418   https://www.upi.com/Top_News/US/2017/01/03/Nomination-expires-for-Obama-Supreme-Court-appointee-Merrick-Garland/4841483472115/

419   https://slate.com/news-and-politics/2016/03/merrick-garland-would-shift-the-supreme-court-left-a-lot.html

Clinton Email Scandal

Obama's Department of Justice filed a court motion in May 2016 opposing the conservative legal organization Judicial Watch's request for Hillary Clinton to be deposed in an ongoing open records case involving her use of a private server for classified e-mail.[420] Government lawyers wrote in their filing that Judicial Watch was trying to expand the case at hand in a "wholly inappropriate" manner before depositions would be finished in a separate case involving the same private server.

The previous month, Obama had indicated in an interview that he saw no merit in possible criminal charges being pressed against his one-time secretary of state in the matter. He attempted to justify Clinton's actions by saying that she had demonstrated "carelessness," at the very worst, by utilizing an unofficial, inadequately encrypted email system for State Department communication.[421] He insisted that she had not jeopardized national security when she improperly transmitted a huge amount of classified information. Obama argued that his otherwise "outstanding" former secretary had not intended to hurt the country.

Others suggested that Clinton's actions were a criminal matter, in violation of the Espionage Act, specifically section 793, subsections (d) and (e) regarding willful retention or transmission of classified information. In a questionable and much debated turn of events, the FBI found that while Clinton was "extremely careless" in handling classified information, it did not believe her transgressions amounted to "gross negligence" and therefore did not warrant criminal charges.[422]

---

420 https://www.nytimes.com/2015/03/03/us/politics/hillary-clintons-use-of-private-email-at-state-department-raises-flags.html; https://thehill.com/policy/national-security/281565-feds-fight-to-prevent-clinton-deposition-in-email-case

421 https://www.chicagotribune.com/bal-obama-puts-his-thumb-on-the-scale-for-hillary-20160414-story.html

422 https://www.wired.com/2016/07/fbi-director-clinton-emails-careless-not-criminal/

This decision, Glenn Greenwald noted, reveals a double standard in the application of the Espionage Act. Greenwald agreed that Clinton's actions did not constitute criminality; but, he pointed out "this case does not exist in isolation. It exists in a political climate where secrecy is regarded as the highest end, where people have their lives destroyed for the most trivial—or, worse, the most well-intentioned—violations of secrecy laws, even in the absence of any evidence of harm or malignant intent."[423] To take just one of the eight whistleblowers Obama charged under the Espionage Act, "Chelsea Manning was charged with multiple felonies and faced decades in prison for leaking documents that she firmly believed the public had the right to see; unlike the documents Clinton recklessly mishandled, *none of those was top secret.*"

423 https://theintercept.com/2016/07/05/washington-has-been-obsessed-with-punishing-secrecy-violations-until-hillary-clinton/; also see https://www.theguardian.com/us-news/2015/mar/16/obama-double-standard-petraeus-leaks

Kissinger

In May 2016 at the Pentagon, Obama's Secretary of Defense Ashton Carter honored former secretary of state Henry Kissinger with the Distinguished Public Service Award. Kissinger had served in public office from 1969 to 1977. By general consensus, even among his supporters, he managed to do a great deal of damage. As New York University history professor Greg Grandin put it in the *Nation*, "Kissinger is implicated in at least three genocides (Cambodia, Bangladesh, and East Timor) and, give or take, 4 million deaths."[424]

Kissinger admirers list as his chief accomplishments his opening of the gates to a hermetic China, as well as his impact on improved relations with the Soviet Union, which included an arms limitation treaty. This is balanced by his instigation of some of the century's worst atrocities. "Carpet-bombing Cambodia, supporting Pakistan's genocide in Bangladesh, greenlighting the Argentinian dictatorship, murderous crackdown on dissidents—all of those were Kissinger initiatives, all pushed in the name of pursuing American national interests and fighting communism," wrote *Vox*.[425]

The bombing of Cambodia killed between 150,000 and 500,000 civilians. The crucial support given to the Pinochet regime in Chile led to the deaths of thousands.[426] The invasion of East Timor, sanctioned and propped up at Kissinger's behest, killed at least 100,000 Timorese.[427] The worst bloodbath as a result of the strategy orchestrated by Kissinger under the auspices of "strategic necessity" involved the 1971 declaration of independence of Bangladesh from Pakistan. The Pakistanis, supported by Kissinger and the State Department, tried to

424   https://www.thenation.com/article/the-obama-administration-just-granted-henry-kissinger-a-distinguished-public-service-award/
425   https://www.vox.com/2016/5/9/11640562/kissinger-pentagon-award
426   https://nsarchive2.gwu.edu/NSAEBB/NSAEBB437/; https://www.globalpolicy.org/component/content/article/165/29544.html
427   https://www.wsws.org/en/articles/2001/12/kiss-d19.html

suppress independence by perpetrating a laundry list of war crimes, including massive numbers of rapes and indiscriminate murder. In all, it is estimated that 3 million people were killed in the process.[428]

Despite this, some forty years later, Kissinger received the Pentagon award from the Obama administration. Separately, Vice President Biden expressed his admiration for the man he called "a friend—a genuine friend," in a 2016 address before the World Jewish Congress.[429] He fawned, "Over the years, I profited by his friendship, by his wisdom, the incredible breadth of knowledge he possesses, I would argue, unlike any other leader in the world today. He doesn't have a rival, in my view, in the entire world."

PART V

Asset Forfeiture

With no fanfare, Attorney General Loretta Lynch in 2016 reinstated the Department of Justice's Equitable Sharing Program, which gives local authorities the incentive to take advantage of asset forfeiture laws.[430]

These laws allow law enforcement agencies to seize property they believe to be somehow related to criminal activity. No trial or due process beyond mere suspicion is necessary, and the bounty is shared with federal authorities.

The Equitable Sharing Program, which was suspended briefly in 2015 due to budget cuts, gives local law enforcement agencies leeway to circumnavigate state government and take direct advantage of federal forfeiture rules. These laws disproportionately negatively affect the poor. People who lack the connections or financial means to pursue the return of their property are left out in the cold.

Horror stories abound: a family with two small children traveling across Texas had cash seized from their car with no reason given.[431] The life savings of a twenty-two-year-old traveling to California to pursue a career in the entertainment industry was taken.[432] The owner of a barbecue restaurant had $17,000 confiscated after his car was stopped.[433] The resulting cash squeeze forced him to shut down his restaurant. None of these victims were ever charged with a crime.

Public indignation over these unwarranted intrusions by the Obama administration into private property led some states, including Pennsylvania and Tennessee, to pass laws designed to thwart asset forfeiture without due process.

430 https://www.usnews.com/opinion/articles/2016-04-11/obamas-doj-sets-back-justice-with-asset-forfeiture-program
431 https://www.newyorker.com/magazine/2013/08/12/taken
432 http://www.huffingtonpost.com/2015/05/07/dea-asset-forfeiture-joseph-rivers_n_7231744.html
433 https://www.washingtonpost.com/sf/investigative/2014/09/06/stop-and-seize/

To his credit, Republican Governor Rick Scott of Florida steered through his state legislature one of the most effective judicial responses to asset forfeiture. The law simply states that no asset seizure can take place unless the victim has been charged with a crime. Even this self-described hard-on-crime conservative found asset confiscation without minimal due process too unfair for his taste.

This was not the case with Obama, who not only did nothing about asset confiscation but made matters worse. A 2015 report by the Institute for Justice showed that the amount of money in the combined asset forfeiture funds of the Department of Justice and the U.S. Treasury tripled from less than $1.5 billion in 2008, the year Obama was elected, to roughly $4.5 billion in 2014.[434]

Asset forfeiture law, intended to target drug kingpins, dates back to the 1970s. But it wasn't until the Reagan-era War on Drugs that federal agents were granted nearly unlimited powers to seize assets, including real estate, from private citizens. This was in no small part due to the efforts of Senator Joe Biden, who in 1981 commissioned a government report to examine why asset forfeiture was not more widely used to fight crime.[435] As a result, Biden and Senator Strom Thurmond (R-SC) spearheaded the 1984 Comprehensive Crime Control Act, which lowered the burden of proof for asset seizures. Agents now had only to *believe* that what they were seizing was of equal value to money *believed* to have stemmed from drug sales. It also allowed police to seize and absorb a person's property without proving the person guilty of a crime, and created the "equitable sharing" program, which enabled local and state law enforcement to retain up to 80 percent of assets seized.[436]

---

434 https://ij.org/wp-content/uploads/2015/11/policing-for-profit-2nd-edition.pdf; https://thecrimereport.org/2015/11/10/2015-11-civil-asset-forfeiture-report/
435 https://www.gao.gov/assets/140/133043.pdf; https://www.washingtonexaminer.com/news/civil-libertarians-have-a-beef-with-joe-biden-over-asset-forfeiture
436 https://fee.org/articles/how-a-young-joe-biden-became-the-architect-of-the-governments-asset-forfeiture-program/

The Democratic Party expects progressives to hold their noses and vote for pseudo-egalitarians who outwardly decry the powers of Wall Street and the Military Industrial Complex, while these paragons of equality see to it that not one errant banker from the crash of 2007 is sent to jail, and that not one of the multi-billion-, or even trillion-, dollar military boondoggles like the F-35 are halted.

Obama and Biden progressive? Progressively more cautious, centrist, and incremental over the course of their time in the White House—that is, a time when we had (and continue to have) a twenty-trillion-dollar monkey on our backs, the national debt.

Clinton Foundation

Top figures at the U.S. Department of Justice denied a 2016 request by the FBI to expand and intensify an investigation into possible corruption at the Clinton Foundation.[437] The FBI earlier in the year had sought to open up a criminal conflict of interest case after a bank had informed the agency of suspicious activity in certain accounts associated with a foreign contributor to the foundation. At the time of the questionable activity, Hillary Clinton was secretary of state.

The FBI met with top officials and lower-ranking field officers of the DOJ. The latter insisted that a case probing public corruption at the foundation should be opened, while the upper-level officials argued against it, and ultimately quashed it.

---

437 https://edition.cnn.com/2016/08/11/politics/hillary-clinton-state-department-clinton-foundation/index.html; https://edition.cnn.com/2016/08/11/politics/hillary-clinton-cgi-cheryl-mills/index.html

Clemency

The U.S. Constitution enables the president to grant both pardons and reprieves to people convicted of federal offenses, and to commute sentences imposed for such crimes. These acts of mercy are collectively called clemency.

A presidential pardon allows someone convicted of a federal crime to be absolved or forgiven of it and to never be liable for any new prosecutions or remaining penalties related to the crime. The public record of the conviction is wiped away. On the other hand, a presidential reprieve postpones a sentence or penalty. A commutation is the lessening of a penalty or sentence. Another presidential act of clemency is remission, which is relief from a forfeiture or restitution order that has been imposed.

During the course of his two terms in the presidential office, Barack Obama exercised his constitutional right to grant executive clemency to 1,927 people convicted of federal crimes.[438] Of these, 1,715 were commutations and 212 were pardons. Many were for drug-related offenses, and virtually all of the offenders were convicted of non-violent crimes. Not since Truman had a president granted so many clemencies. But nor had any president on record received remotely as many clemency requests as Obama. Over the full course of his presidency, Obama received an unprecedented 36,544 petitions for clemency. Therefore, he granted only 5 percent of the requests. By contrast, every president from Theodore Roosevelt to Jimmy Carter granted more than 20 percent of their clemency requests—except one. The only president who granted a lower rate of requests than Obama was George W. Bush, who granted just 2 percent.

Part of the reason Obama received so many petitions for clemency was his Justice Department's 2014 Clemency Initiative, which

---

438   https://www.pewresearch.org/fact-tank/2017/01/20/obama-used-more-clemency-power/

encouraged non-violent federal offenders to petition the president for a commutation of their sentences, particularly if the likely penalty or sentence at the time of the Initiative's implementation were milder than the penalty imposed at the time of the petitioner's conviction. In total, more than 24,000 offenders responded to the Initiative. Of the 1,928 grants of clemency made by Obama, 1,696 were sentence commutations under the Clemency Initiative.[439] Despite this, by the end of Obama's second term, there were 2,687 non-violent drug trafficking offenders who had been incarcerated when the Clemency Initiative was announced and who appeared to meet all of the commutation criteria, yet only 92 (3.4 percent) of them received clemency from Obama, leaving 2,595 offenders who did not obtain relief.

439   https://www.ussc.gov/research/research-reports/analysis-implementation-2014-clemency-initiative

Dreamers

From the start of his campaign into the waning days of his presidency, Obama promised immigration reform including legal protection for 800,000 young "dreamers," undocumented immigrants who came to the U.S. as children. He fell far short of that goal. Even with Democrats controlling both houses of Congress during his first two years in office, Obama could not protect the dreamers. By the end of his two terms as president, he had deported more people from the U.S. than had all other presidents of the twentieth century combined.[440]

Obama claimed that "actual threats to our security" were the focus of his administration's efforts. "Criminals, not children," he said.[441]

Yet, among the many deportees were hundreds of children of Cambodian refugees, sent "back home" to an utterly foreign country many had never visited, much less lived in, because of relatively minor or early infractions. "I had no luggage. I had about $150 in my pocket. No possessions at all," recalled one such person, tossed out for credit card fraud.[442] "Everything was different, it was like a culture shock. The environment is different, the people are different, the language is different," said another, who had shot a gun into the air when he was fifteen. "Some don't make it," said Bill Herod, an American who worked with the deportees in Cambodia. "We've had suicides."

When Obama visited a 2013 fundraiser in California for the Democratic National Committee, he was derided by protesters as the "Deporter-in-Chief."[443] Immigration activists continued to demand accountability from him years later, in the months leading up to the

440 https://abcnews.go.com/Politics/obamas-deportation-policy-numbers/story?id=41715661

441 https://obamawhitehouse.archives.gov/the-press-office/2014/11/20/remarks-president-address-nation-immigration

442 https://www.pbs.org/newshour/show/deported-u-s-cambodians-fight-immigration-policy

443 https://www.foxnews.com/politics/deporter-in-chief-president-obamas-base-turning-against-him-over-inaction-on-immigration

2020 presidential election. "There's still a distrust factor," said Domingo Garcia, president of the League of United Latin American Citizens, at a 2019 convention where members called on Democratic hopefuls to speak out against Obama's mass deportations.[444] "Obama promised to pass immigration reform in the first 100 days of his administration. It didn't happen," he said. Cecilia Garcia, a U.S. citizen, attended the convention to protest the deportation of her husband in 2012 after he was pulled over for an expired license plate, despite not having a criminal background or a pending deportation order.

When asked in 2011, during a Univision Latino youth town hall, about granting formal administrative relief to undocumented youth, Obama gave the subject short shrift. "There are enough laws on the books by Congress that are very clear in terms of how we have to enforce our immigration system that for me to simply, through executive order, ignore those congressional mandates would not conform with my appropriate role as president," he said.[445]

The following year, expressing frustration over Congress's failure to give the dreamers a path to citizenship, Obama issued an executive order to extend the dreamers' work authorization and deportation relief.[446] The constitutionality of this action, given its open-endedness and Congress' repeated rejection of similar legislation, was widely called into question. Nearly 800,000 people were ultimately approved for Obama's Deferred Action for Childhood Arrivals (DACA) program.[447]

As he prepared to turn the presidency over to Donald Trump, immigration advocates urged Obama to make immigration protections more permanent. Some issued pleas for Obama to grant pardons

444 https://www.buzzfeednews.com/article/nidhiprakash/ice-deportations-obama-trump

445 https://unitedwedream.org/2011/05/obama-continues-to-deport-dreamers/

446 https://www.dhs.gov/deferred-action-childhood-arrivals-daca

447 https://www.theguardian.com/us-news/2017/sep/05/donald-trump-dreamers-program-young-immigrants

to all DACA recipients. "He's got to do something for them other than to simply say, 'Oh, I talked to the president-elect and told him it would be an unwise idea,'" Rep. Luis Gutierrez (D-Ill), said. "Do more. Gather them together. Use the bully pulpit to show who they are. Call them together. Do more. He's not doing enough."[448]

President Trump terminated DACA in September 2017, throwing the fates of hundreds of thousands of young undocumented migrants into uncertainty.[449]

448 https://www.huffingtonpost.co.uk/entry/obama-daca-dreamers_n_58593f7ce4b0b3
ddfd8ea15b
449 https://www.theguardian.com/us-news/2017/sep/05/donald-trump-dreamers-
program-young-immigrants; https://time.com/5670018/daca-rescinded-dreamers/

PART VI

SOCIAL POLICY

Test Scores

In the waning days of the Great Recession, President Obama and his education secretary Arne Duncan announced the creation of a $4.35 billion grant program called Race to the Top.[450] States had to agree to adopt new college and career-ready standards in order to apply for the sorely needed grant money, which was offered as part of the American Recovery and Reinvestment Act, aka The Stimulus. The administration also put $350 million toward developing tests aligned to the new standards. The 2009 move followed tremendous backlash to pre-Obama Common Core math and language arts requirements set forth in the earlier No Child Left Behind law. Education agencies and governors in forty-six states and the District of Columbia applied for the Obama grant money.

"States didn't have to adopt, but they knew that doing so would help their cause," wrote NPR. "The administration used the money to encourage—Obama's critics would say coerce—states to embrace its education policies."[451]

The fast-tracking of Common Core standards was a major priority of the program, which Obama said in his announcement would make the American education system the envy of the world:

> "I'm issuing a challenge to our nation's governors, to school boards and principals and teachers, to businesses and non-for-profits, to parents and students: if you set and enforce rigorous and challenging standards and assessments; if you put outstanding teachers at the front of the classroom; if you turn around failing schools – your state can win a Race to the Top grant that will not only help students outcompete workers around the world, but let them fulfill their God-given potential."[452]

450 https://obamawhitehouse.archives.gov/issues/education/k-12/race-to-the-top
451 https://www.npr.org/sections/ed/2017/01/13/500421608/obamas-impact-on-americas-schools
452 https://web.archive.org/web/20100305055547/https://www.whitehouse.gov/the_press_office/Remarks-by-the-President-at-the-Department-of-Education/

Nearly a decade later, the average ACT math score reached a twenty-year low.[453] Students' math achievement for the graduating class of 2018 was 20.5, marking a steady decline from 20.9 five years before, and virtually no progress since 1998, when it was 20.6, according to Education Week. "We're at a very dangerous point. And if we do nothing, it will keep on declining," said ACT's chief executive officer, Marten Roorda. The average ACT English score for the class of 2018 was 20.2, the same as five years before, and down half a point from 2007. SAT scores in math, critical reading, and writing all dropped from 2009 to 2016, until the College Board fully implemented a new version of the test, tailored to Common Core.[454]

453   https://www.edweek.org/ew/articles/2018/10/17/math-scores-slide-to-a-20-year-low. html

454   https://www.theatlantic.com/education/archive/2015/01/new-sat-new-problems/ 384596/; https://www.reuters.com/investigates/special-report/college-sat-coleman/

Tax Code Simplification

On his first Tax Day as president, April 15, 2009, Barack Obama proclaimed: "We need to simplify a monstrous tax code that is far too complicated for most Americans to understand, but just complicated enough for the insiders who know how to game the system."[455]

Indeed, from the time of his inauguration three months earlier, Obama had promised sweeping changes to simplify the labyrinthine federal tax code. Hopes for an overhaul were stoked by the fact that both political parties—while disagreeing on the substance of tax policy—agreed that something had to be done to ease the code's complexity. This complexity extends to the inability of many individuals to take advantage of the Earned Income Tax Credit, Saver's Credit, the Child Tax Credit, and the American Opportunity Credit.[456]

Federal tax-code compliance utilizes more than 6 billion hours annually.[457] This is the equivalent of 3 million people working 2,000 hours each, or full-time, on tax preparation. The federal tax code totals approximately 75,000 pages, and is chockful of goodies for special interests that take up considerable chunks of its verbiage.[458] Former president Jimmy Carter called the code "a disgrace to the human race" in 1976.[459] At the time, it covered about 25,000 pages.

455 https://obamawhitehouse.archives.gov/the-press-office/remarks-president-taxes-41509

456 https://review.chicagobooth.edu/public-policy/2018/article/why-it-s-so-hard-simplify-tax-code

457 https://www.ntu.org/foundation/detail/study-2338-billion-61-billion-hours-lost-to-rising-tax-complexity

458 https://www.washingtonexaminer.com/look-at-how-many-pages-are-in-the-federal-tax-code

459 https://www.jimmycarterlibrary.gov/assets/documents/speeches/acceptance_speech.pdf

"It's going to take time to undo the damage of years of carve-outs and loopholes," Obama promised. "But I want every American to know that we will rewrite the tax code so that it puts your interests over any special interests. And we'll make it easier, quicker and less expensive for you to file a return, so that April 15th is not a date that is approached with dread every year."[460] Nothing of the sort happened.

460 https://obamawhitehouse.archives.gov/the-press-office/remarks-president-taxes-41509

Obamacare

The Affordable Care Act was signed into law on March 23, 2010 by President Obama, but full benefits offered by individual and family health plans under the ACA did not come into effect until 2014. From 2013 to early 2017, health insurance premiums for an individual not receiving subsidies rose from $197 per month to $393 per month. Over the same time frame, premiums for a family not receiving subsidies climbed from $426 per month to $1,021 per month.[461]

Throughout the Obama years, the proportion of Americans under the age of sixty-five having high-deductible plans under ACA rose from less than 30 percent to nearly 40 percent.[462] On the whole, then, coverage went down while premiums went up.

The number of uninsured Americans declined from 48 million in 2010 to 28 million in 2016.[463] Yet in December 2017, Republicans in Congress repealed the ACA's individual mandate, a provision which required most U.S. residents to have health insurance and imposed penalties on those who did not comply.[464] At the time, the Congressional Budget Office estimated that, as a result of repealing the mandate, 22 million people would lose coverage by 2026, leaving 50 million Americans uninsured, not far from the 48 million uninsured in 2010.[465]

Progressives like Bernie Sanders, who support a single-payer plan as an alternative to Obamacare, point out that it would lead to the

461 https://news.ehealthinsurance.com/news/average-individual-health-insurance-premiums-increased-99-since-2013-the-year-before-obamacare-family-premiums-increased-140-according-to-ehealth-com-shopping-data

462 https://www.cdc.gov/nchs/data/nhis/earlyrelease/ERHDHP_Access_0617.pdf

463 https://money.cnn.com/2017/03/13/news/economy/uninsured-rate-obamacare/index.html

464 https://www.vox.com/policy-and-politics/2017/11/14/16651698/obamacare-individual-mandate-republican-tax-bill

465 https://www.cbo.gov/system/files/115th-congress-2017-2018/costestimate/52941-hr1628bcra.pdf

effective elimination of private insurers. His Medicare for All program promised to provide everyone in America with comprehensive health care coverage, free at the point of service.[466] The difference between the two plans is an extra $1,375 in additional insurance administrative costs per newly insured individual per year from 2014 to 2022 under Obamacare, as compared to single-payer.[467] Overall, the insurance overhead equals 22.5 percent of estimated ACA expenditures by the federal government of $2.76 trillion during the eight-year period. By contrast, the single-payer Medicare program has an overhead of just 2 percent. When Medicare was enacted in 1965, virtually everyone aged sixty-five and over was made eligible for its benefits within a year, without the aid of sophisticated computers.[468] Despite pressure from Medicare for All activists in the run-up to the 2020 presidential election, former vice president Joe Biden, like Obama, opposed a single-payer model.[469]

The ACA plans suffer from low coverage (although they do, to their credit, continue to cover pre-existing conditions in most cases, as does the single-payer plan) as well as restricted networks. In the first half of 2020, 43.4 percent of U.S. adults ages nineteen to sixty-four were inadequately insured, according to the Commonwealth Fund's Biennial Health Insurance Survey.[470] Meanwhile, among high-income countries, the U.S. dedicates the highest proportion of its economy to health care, at around 17 percent of GDP, but its life expectancy is among the lowest.[471]

466 https://berniesanders.com/issues/medicare-for-all/
467 https://www.healthaffairs.org/do/10.1377/hblog20150527.047928/full/
468 https://www.ssa.gov/history/pdf/ThirtyYearsPopulation.pdf
469 https://www.politico.com/news/2020/04/25/biden-health-care-left-207639
470 https://www.commonwealthfund.org/publications/issue-briefs/2020/aug/looming-crisis-health-coverage-2020-biennial
471 https://www.commonwealthfund.org/publications/issue-briefs/2020/jan/us-health-care-global-perspective-2019; https://stats.oecd.org/Index.aspx?DataSetCode=HEALTH_STAT

A 2019 survey by West Health and Gallup found that Americans had borrowed $88 billion in the previous year to pay for health care.[472] Nearly half said they feared bankruptcy in the event of a major health event, and one in four had skipped a medical treatment because of cost. In 2020, insurance companies could require families to pay as much as $16,300 and individuals to pay as much as $8,150 in out-of-pocket costs.[473] That was up from $7,900 for an individual and $15,800 for a family in 2019.

The future of Obamacare is unclear. In December 2019, the 5th U.S. Circuit Court of Appeals declared the Affordable Care Act's individual mandate unconstitutional, while sending back to a lower court the question of whether the entire law can remain without it. The case was heard by the Supreme Court in November 2020. A ruling was expected around June 2021.[474]

---

472 https://news.gallup.com/poll/248129/westhealth-gallup-us-healthcare-cost-crisis-press-release.aspx

473 https://www.healthcare.gov/glossary/out-of-pocket-maximum-limit/

474 https://www.npr.org/sections/health-shots/2020/09/21/915000375/the-future-of-the-affordable-care-act-in-a-supreme-court-without-ginsburg

Tax Cuts Retained

Obama campaigned on raising tax rates for couples earning more than $250,000 a year, and individuals earning more than $200,000 a year. Under Bush, the top rate was cut from 39.6 percent annually to 35 percent. Obama pledged again and again to restore the highest tax bracket rate to 39.6 percent, as it had been under Clinton. But in 2010, after he was elected, Obama relented to a two-year extension of the lower rate of 35 percent for the most affluent earners.[475] This was the outcome of a "deal" reached between Vice President Biden and Senator Mitch McConnell that, according to Branko Marcetic, *Jacobin* staff writer and author of *Yesterday's Man: The Case Against Joe Biden*, "outraged Democrats across the political spectrum".[476] Marcetic explains:

> "In exchange for keeping unemployment insurance alive for another thirteen months, extending an education tax credit for two more years, and an eleventh-hour stimulus of payroll tax cuts, Biden gave McConnell not just two more years of high-income tax cuts, but a lower estate tax with a higher exemption, new tax write-offs for businesses, and a maximum 15 percent capital gains tax rate locked in for two years."

Finally, at the start of 2013, Obama was able to raise rates back to 39.6 percent on couples making more than $450,000 ($400,000 for individuals) a year. But those making between $250,000 ($200,000) and the highest threshold of $450,000 ($400,000) were able to retain the tax cuts initiated by Bush, leaving their rate at 35 percent, nearly 5 percent lower than it was under Clinton.[477]

475 https://www.politifact.com/truth-o-meter/promises/obameter/promise/38/repeal-the-bush-tax-cuts-for-higher-incomes/

476 https://jacobinmag.com/2020/02/joe-biden-history-republicans-tax-cuts-barack-obama-yesterdays-man

477 https://www.politifact.com/truth-o-meter/promises/obameter/promise/1/increase-the-capital-gains-and-dividends-taxes-for/

For 77 percent of American households, the deal translated into higher federal taxes that year, according to an analysis by the Tax Policy Center, a nonpartisan Washington research group.[478] Households earnings between $40,000 and $50,000 a year would face an average tax increase of $579, and those making between $50,000 and $75,000 annually would see an average hike of $822, the group estimated.

478 https://eu.usatoday.com/story/money/business/2013/01/02/taxes-rise-for-most-americans/1803773/

Medical Marijuana

In July 2013, a number of raucous raids by Federal agents on medical marijuana dispensaries were carried out in the Puget Sound vicinity of Washington state.[479] As the armed government agents came through the door, one owner thought he was being robbed while another said he felt humiliated as he and his staff were ordered to lie face down with their hands behind heads and guns pointed at them.

The decision concerning which dispensaries to raid in order to enforce federal laws prohibiting medical marijuana use was called "willy-nilly," "arbitrary," and "inscrutable" by some of the targets.[480] Raids had already taken place in 2011 on twenty dispensaries in Washington state, with the DEA claiming to have evidence that they were fronts for commercial drug dealing.[481] Four of these were raided again in 2013 despite no criminal charges being brought against them.

Americans for Safe Access, a medical marijuana advocacy group, claimed that by mid-2013, the Obama administration had spent more than $300 million on enforcing the federal statutes covering the prohibition of medical marijuana use.[482] At the time, according to a CBS poll, 86 percent of Americans favored legalizing medical marijuana.[483] What did Obama have to gain acting against the beliefs of 86 percent of the population? The president could have easily muzzled an overzealous Drug Enforcement Agency administrator. Why did he not?

In August 2013, a new policy was articulated in what became known as the Cole Memo, published through the Justice

479 https://www.theatlantic.com/national/archive/2013/07/feds-raid-pot-dispenaries-washington-where-drug-legal/312915/
480 https://www.vice.com/en/article/ex5j9m/dea-ignores-state-laws-in-washington-raids-dispensaries
481 https://komonews.com/archive/raided-marijuana-dispensaries-had-been-targeted-before
482 https://www.huffingtonpost.co.uk/entry/obama-medical-marijuana_n_3437636
483 https://www.cbsnews.com/news/majority-of-americans-now-support-legal-pot-poll-says/

Department.[484] It provided that states that had legalized marijuana were expected to adhere to strict regulatory oversight and, if they did so, could reasonably expect to be left alone by the federal authorities. Sporadic raids persisted, but at a much lower volume than prior to the memo.

Nevertheless, in 2016, when a Pew poll showed a solid, 57 percent majority of Americans favoring legalization of marijuana outright—not just for medical purposes—Obama announced that marijuana would remain a Schedule 1 drug, sharing that ignoble position with heroin.[485] This included marijuana for medical use.

At the same time, research opportunities on the plant's potentially curative properties were expanded. Yet, at the end of Obama's presidency thousands of non-violent pot prisoners continued to languish in jails and marijuana remained a Schedule 1 drug.

484 https://www.justice.gov/iso/opa/resources/3052013829132756857467.pdf
485 https://www.pewresearch.org/fact-tank/2016/10/12/support-for-marijuana-legalization-continues-to-rise/

Social Security

The 2014 Farm Bill, signed into law by President Obama, included legislation to cut $8.7 billion in food stamp benefits, amounting to 850,000 households losing an average of $90 per month.[486] The reduction would eliminate so-called "Heat and Eat" policies used in fifteen states and Washington D.C. to cut out paperwork and claim additional food stamp benefits for people with low incomes. The food stamp cut was opposed by a number of progressive Democrats in the House who expected them to disproportionately affect the elderly and disabled.

In the majority of states, people who spent more than half their income on housing and utilities were eligible for deductions which increased their food stamp benefit levels. In order to claim the deduction, they had to show state agencies their housing and utility bills. In "Heat and Eat" states, however, anyone who qualified for energy assistance was assumed to also qualify for the housing deduction. As a result, someone who qualified for as little as $1 in energy assistance through the Low-Income Home Energy Assistance Program (LIHEAP) was eligible for more food stamp benefits. Under the new law, families would be required to receive more than $20 in LIHEAP benefits to qualify for "Heat and Eat."

Caryn Long, director of the food bank coalition Feeding Pennsylvania, pointed out that "Heat and Eat" policies benefited those who already qualified for both food stamps and energy assistance. "They may be receiving a minimal benefit not because they're not eligible for more, but because federal funding for the LIHEAP program has been significantly cut," she told MSNBC.[487]

Over the previous three years, the federal government had steadily reduced total appropriations for winter heating by about

486 https://www.msnbc.com/msnbc/obama-signs-food-stamp-cut-msna263456
487 https://www.msnbc.com/all/food-stamp-users-face-another-hit-msna243166

one-third, causing an estimated 300,000 families to lose home energy assistance.[488]

Only two months prior to the Farm Bill proposal, the 47 million recipients of food stamps were socked with an automatic $5 billion reduction in their benefits.[489] The shifting winds marked an apparent departure for a president who had campaigned in both 2008 and 2012 to protect the Social Security program and to reject any plans to cut benefits. "But shortly after re-election in 2012," noted the *Intercept*, "the Obama Administration proposed re-calculating the way Social Security's cost of living adjustments work."[490]

In his April 2013 budget, Obama included $1.2 trillion worth of spending cuts that included slashing Social Security benefits.[491] He had proposed the cuts partly as a compromise to break a fiscal deadlock in Washington. In response, protesters gathered outside the White House to deliver a petition signed by 2.3 million people in opposition to the move.

According to the *Guardian*: "a growing number of Obama's supporters on the left fear the concession will act as a permanent line in the sand, making it impossible to resist future pressure to reduce spending on welfare. In particular, they are angry at the president's proposal to link further increases in social security to a less generous measure of inflation, known as the 'chained' consumer price index, or CPI."[492] The advocacy group Social Security Works estimated that under the

488 https://www.msnbc.com/all/no-money-no-heat-no-help-msna242101

489 https://www.cbpp.org/research/snap-benefits-will-be-cut-for-nearly-all-participants-in-november-2013; https://www.msnbc.com/all/americas-new-hunger-crisis-msna190131

490 https://theintercept.com/2016/06/02/obama-wanted-to-cut-social-security-then-bernie-sanders-happened/

491 https://www.theguardian.com/world/2013/apr/09/obama-welfare-risk-budget-proposal

492 https://www.theguardian.com/world/2013/apr/09/obama-welfare-risk-budget-proposal

chained CPI, a person age seventy-five would receive a yearly benefit $653 lower after ten years.[493]

Pressure was brought to bear as well by Senator Bernie Sanders, who mobilized a coalition of organizations, including women's rights groups and labor unions, to oppose chained CPI. "Under this intense activist pressure, the White House was unable to convince its own allies in Congress that this change was worth the political costs," wrote the *Intercept*.[494] "The next year, the chained CPI was quietly dropped from Obama's budget proposal."

In 2016, Obama finally endorsed an expansion of Social Security for the first time. He argued that the increased benefits could be paid for "by asking the wealthiest Americans to contribute a little bit more. They can afford it. I can afford it."[495] The *Intercept* suggested this arose out of the efforts of Sanders from 2014 to advocate for a lifting of Social Security's payroll tax cap so that wealthier people paid more into the system, and then increasing benefits to seniors.

493 https://archives.cjr.org/united_states_project/the_media_discover_the_chained.
     php?page=2
494 https://theintercept.com/2016/06/02/obama-wanted-to-cut-social-security-then-
     bernie-sanders-happened/
495 https://www.vox.com/2016/6/1/11835510/obama-expand-social-security

Militarization of Federal Agencies

A widely disseminated 2016 report by OpentheBooks.com, *The Militarization of America: Non-military Federal Agencies Purchases of Guns, Ammo, and Military-style Equipment,* stated that "administrative agencies including the Food and Drug Administration, Small Business Administration, Smithsonian Institution, Social Security Administration, National Oceanic and Atmospheric Administration, United States Mint, Department of Education, Bureau of Engraving and Printing, National Institute of Standards and Technology, and many other agencies" receive guns and other weapons, both lethal and non-lethal, from the federal government or purchase them on the open market.[496]

According to the report, which detailed purchases made over an eight-year period from fiscal years 2006 to 2014, "The Animal and Plant Health Inspection Service spent $4.77 million purchasing shotguns, .308 caliber rifles, night vision goggles, propane cannons, liquid explosives, pyro supplies, buckshot, LP gas cannons, drones, remote controlled helicopters, thermal cameras, military waterproof thermal infrared scopes, and more."

Report author Adam Andrzejewski explained: "As the Obama administration and its allies are pushing hard for an assault weapons ban on private citizens, taxpayers are asking why IRS agents need AR-15s. After grabbing legal power, federal bureaucrats are amassing firepower. It's time to scale back the federal arsenal."[497]

The sixty-seven agencies plus fifteen Cabinet-level departments covered in the report, which exclude traditional law enforcement agencies like the DEA and the ATF, had in aggregate over 200,000

---

496 https://www.openthebooks.com/assets/1/7/Oversight_TheMilitarizationOf America_06102016.pdf

497 https://www.forbes.com/sites/adamandrzejewski/2016/06/21/an-assault-weapons-ban-for-the-irs-and-other-federal-regulatory-agencies/#2c97dc673b9e

employees with the authority to carry firearms. This exceeded the entire work force of the Marine Corps, with 182,000 personnel. Traditional law enforcement agencies like the FBI together spent only 77 percent of what the non-law enforcement agencies spent on weapons in the same period.

With regard to the IRS, Andrzejewski wrote that *its "stockpile includes pump-action and semi-automatic shotguns with buckshot and slugs; and semi-automatic AR-15 rifles (S&W M&P 15) and military-style H&K 416 rifles."* Other equipment purchased by these agencies include paintballs, Tasers, projectiles, unmanned aircraft, grenades/launchers, and buckshot. The report also found that federal agencies had spent $313,958 on paintball equipment, along with $14.7 million on Tasers, $1.6 million on unmanned aircraft, $8.2 million on buckshot, $7.44 million on projectiles, and $4 million on grenades/launchers.

The Food and Drug Administration alone had 183 armed "special agents." The U.S. Geological Survey, which aims to provide "real-time data and information on current conditions and earth observations," spent $1.33 million on guns, ammunition, and military-style equipment.[498] Other agencies purchasing weaponry included the Department of Agriculture, the Railroad Retirement Board, the Tennessee Valley Authority, the Office of Personnel Management, the Consumer Product Safety Commission, and the U.S. Fish and Wildlife Service.

498 https://www.usgs.gov/

Drug Overdose Crisis

Drug overdose deaths in America climbed from a 2008 figure of 11.9 people per 100,000 to 19.8 per 100,000 in 2016 (both figures age-adjusted).[499] In terms of raw numbers, there were 63,632 drug overdose fatalities in 2016 as compared with 36,450 in 2008. This is a sobering increase of more than 40 percent under Obama's leadership. Deaths due to overdoses on synthetic opioids alone (excluding methadone) doubled between 2015 and 2016.[500]

Obama took a characteristically tepid approach to this crisis. As part of Prescription Opioid and Heroin Epidemic Awareness Week in 2016, the administration's measures included: a measured expansion of substance abuse treatment programs; the raising of the limit for buprenorphine patients per doctor; developing measures with the Chinese government "to combat the supply" of fentanyl in the U.S.; as well as "supporting distance learning and telemedicine programs that expand access to healthcare, substance use disorder treatment, and educational opportunities in rural communities."[501] As the statistics demonstrate, Obama's late-to-the-party tactics proved no match for the powerful lure of licit and illicit drugs, particularly opioids and opiates.[502]

Ironically, harsh anti-drug legislation forged by Obama's own vice president appears to have been a major part of the problem. While in the Senate, Joe Biden co-sponsored the Anti-Drug Abuse Act of 1986, a wide-reaching federal effort in the War on Drugs. Among its provisions was the Emergency Crack Control Act, which made overdose prevention sites—safe-injection facilities where people with opioid

---

499   https://www.cdc.gov/nchs/data/databriefs/db294_table.pdf#page=1

500   https://www.cdc.gov/nchs/products/databriefs/db294.htm

501   https://obamawhitehouse.archives.gov/the-press-office/2016/09/19/fact-sheet-obama-administration-announces-prescription-opioid-and-heroin

502   For 2017 and 2018 statistics see https://www.cdc.gov/nchs/products/databriefs/db356.htm

use disorder can consume drugs under medical supervision in order to avoid fatal overdoses—illegal under federal law.[503] It also imposed life imprisonment for any person who distributed drugs resulting in a fatal overdose. "'Biden wrote and passed this law that allowed drug users to be prosecuted as murderers,'" Dr. Carl Hart, Columbia University neuroscientist and chair of the school's department of psychology, told *Politico*.[504] Biden's efforts, according to Hart, "'decrease the likelihood that somebody is gonna help someone who is overdosing.'"

Biden's laws have worsened the opioid epidemic in the very places he claimed to be able to win in his 2020 presidential campaign. It was in Philadelphia, where Biden's campaign was headquartered, that activists and public health workers laid the groundwork in 2018 for what would be the nation's first overdose prevention site. But federal prosecutors filed suit in an effort to block the site from opening, citing the above-mentioned 1986 provision co-sponsored by Biden.[505]

---

503 https://www.congress.gov/bill/99th-congress/senate-bill/2715
504 https://www.politico.com/magazine/story/2019/05/23/joe-biden-2020-drug-war-policies-opioid-crisis-226933
505 https://www.inquirer.com/news/supervised-injection-sites-philadelphia-stop-safehouse-us-attorney-opioid-crisis-20190206.html

GMOs

Flying in the face of 250,000 food safety petitioners, in 2016 Obama signed Senate Bill 764, known in popular parlance as the DARK Act (Deny Americans the Right to Know).[506] The law allows food companies and producers to use QR codes and 1-800 numbers—rather than clear words on packaging to label products that contain genetically modified organisms (GMOs). Obama's action effectively voided many state labeling laws, including one that had recently passed in Vermont.

S. 764 was condemned by groups like the Pesticide Action Network (PAN), which called Obama's decision deeply disappointing. "Billed by its supporters as a 'compromise' on labeling, the DARK Act in fact simply protects the market interests of biotech corporations like Monsanto by shielding them from a public that's increasingly concerned about our food system's over-reliance on genetically engineered (GE) crops and the pesticides they're grown with," Marcia Ishii-Eiteman, senior scientist for PAN, said in a statement.[507] "And by only including QR codes on food packaging, without specific mention of GMOs, this law discriminates against those who don't own smartphones, particularly low-income and rural communities. It would take the same amount of ink—or less—to simply include a label identifying the GE ingredients in the product."

Andy Kimbrell, executive director of the Center for Food Safety, called the decision a "sham and a shame," in another statement.[508] "I don't know what kind of legacy the president hopes to leave, but denying one-third of Americans the right to know what is in the food they feed their families isn't one to be proud of."

---

506 https://www.congress.gov/bill/114th-congress/senate-bill/764/text
507 https://www.panna.org/press-statement/president-obama-signed-bill-undermine-gmo-labeling
508 https://www.centerforfoodsafety.org/press-releases/4438/president-obama-signs-gmo-non-labeling-bill-leaves-millions-of-americans-in-the-dark

Upon leaving office, Obama mused on the potential for genetically engineered food technology after delivering a speech, for which he was reportedly paid $3.26 million, at the Seeds & Chips Global Food Innovation Summit in Milan, Italy.[509] Noting the controversy surrounding the issue, he said the "average person" did not want the government telling him or her what to eat or drink.

"The approach that I took when I was president of the United States is in the same way that I would let the science determine my policies around climate change. I try to let the science determine my attitudes about food production and new technologies," he said in a Q&A following the speech with his former White House chef. "I think it's okay for us to be cautious about how we approach these new technologies and genetic modifications but I don't think we can be closed off to it. I don't think we can be close-minded to it. The truth is, humanity has always engaged in genetic modifications. The rice we eat or the corn we eat or the wheat we eat does not look like what corn or rice or wheat looked like 1,000 years ago."

509 https://geneticliteracyproject.org/2017/05/10/video-obama-gmos-humanity-always-engaged-genetic-modifications/

Unions

Over Labor Day weekend 2016, in his weekly address, Obama lauded labor unions and their historical achievements, including overtime pay, the forty-hour work week, and the minimum wage.[510]

Meantime, unions lobbied furiously against the Obama-backed Trans-Pacific Partnership free trade plan, calling it a gargantuan job killer that would almost solely benefit corporations. As United Steelworkers (USW) president Leo W. Gerard put it, "Currency manipulation is at the heart of this issue, and the passage of the TPP—which doesn't address this global problem—could kill American manufacturing for good."[511]

In his address, the commander in chief asked rhetorically whether Americans "want a future where inequality rises as union membership keeps falling."

Under President Obama, union membership fell from a pathetically low 12.3 percent of all employees in 2009, his first year in office, to an even smaller 10.7 percent membership rate in 2016, scarcely more than one in every ten workers in the United States.[512]

Perhaps this was partially due to what Workforce described as an "inconsistent" relationship between the Obama administration and unions.[513] In 2009, the Obama-backed Employee Free Choice Act failed to pass Congress when Democrats couldn't collect enough votes to defeat a Republican filibuster. Among its proposals, the legislation would have allowed workers to join a union if a majority of employees in a proposed bargaining unit signed on, and stiffened penalties on employers who violated labor laws.

---

510   https://www.youtube.com/watch?v=hKM0TpdWNFo
511   https://aflcio.org/2016/4/19/new-afl-cio-trade-video-warns-tpp-would-double-down-naftas-economic-devastation
512   https://www.districtsentinel.com/latest-data-shows-union-numbers-membership-rate-fell-obama-years/
513   https://www.workforce.com/news/workplace-legacy-barack-obama

The same year, during the bankruptcy and restructuring of GM and Chrysler, "Obama convinced auto industry unions to accept a two-tier wage system that paid entry-level workers significantly less than what they would have made in the past," wrote Workforce.[514] "The deal kept U.S. automakers afloat during the worst of the recession, but was extremely unpopular with workers, dividing union solidarity, and transferring cost-cutting from other industries to manufacturing."

The Affordable Care Act likewise did the president no favors in the eyes of union members. "Thanks to Obamacare's employer mandate and its subsidized insurance exchanges, businesses with fewer than 50 employees now have an incentive to drop health coverage for their employees and let those workers get coverage on the exchanges," wrote *Forbes*.[515] "It's a better deal for those workers, and a better deal for their employers. But it's a big blow to the labor unions who organize the plans, because workers no longer need unions to negotiate or obtain their health coverage."

514 https://www.workforce.com/news/workplace-legacy-barack-obama; https://socialistworker.org/2009/04/06/autoworkers-get-the-stick

515 https://www.forbes.com/sites/theapothecary/2013/09/14/obama-to-labor-unions-multi-employer-health-plans-drop-dead/#2f06e98d9daf

Manufacturing Jobs

From January 2009 to December 2016, the U.S. lost 205,000 manufacturing jobs.[516]

---

516   https://data.bls.gov/timeseries/CES3000000001

Racial Wealth Disparity

In 2016, the average wealth of white families was 6.6 times greater than the average wealth of Black families.[517] The year 2016 can be compared to the year 2010, when wealth was 6.5 times greater for white than for Black families.

The wealth gap remained virtually unchanged the entire time Obama was in office.

---

517   https://apps.urban.org/features/wealth-inequality-charts/

Suicides

The number of suicides in the United States hit 44,965 cases in 2016.[518] This figure represents a nearly 18 percent rise from 2009.[519]

518   https://afsp.org/story/suicide-rate-is-up-1-2-percent-according-to-most-recent-cdc-data-year-2016

519   https://www.cdc.gov/mmwr/preview/mmwrhtml/su6203a31.htm

Race Relations

Three months prior to the inauguration of Donald Trump, a poll was released by CNN/ORC that found that a majority of Americans questioned, 54 percent, felt that race relations had deteriorated under Barack Obama.[520] Incidentally, 86 percent of respondents in the October 2016 poll had a favorable view of their local police, with only 10 percent holding an unfavorable opinion.

Following this, Gallup released a poll in January 2017.[521] Fifty-two percent of those surveyed felt that the United States had lost ground in the area of race relations over the previous eight years. A mere 25 percent of respondents felt that progress had been made. Gallup speculated that a series of tension-producing events during Obama's second term had been largely to blame.

These events began to percolate with the rise of the Black Lives Matter movement from mid-2013 and protests in Ferguson, Missouri the following year. After a grand jury decided in November 2014 not to indict the police officer who shot Michael Brown, Obama observed: "We have made enormous progress in race relations over the past several decades. I've witnessed that in my own life. And to deny that progress, I think, is to deny America's capacity for change."[522]

Obama made similar pronouncements throughout the remainder of his presidency. In December 2014, a Staten Island grand jury declined to indict a white police officer in the case of Eric Garner, an unarmed Black man who died after being subjected to an apparent chokehold during an arrest. Obama said of the grand jury decision: "This is an American problem. When anybody in this country is not

520   https://edition.cnn.com/2016/10/05/politics/obama-race-relations-poll/index.html
521   https://news.gallup.com/poll/201683/americans-assess-progress-obama.aspx
522   https://www.latimes.com/nation/la-na-obama-race-reax-20170816-story.html

being treated equally under the law, that's a problem. And it's my job as president to help solve it."[523]

The July 2016 police shootings of Alton Sterling in Baton Rouge and Philando Castile in Minnesota provoked the following comment by Obama: "all of us as Americans should be troubled by the news. These are not isolated incidents."

The same month, five Dallas police officers were ambushed and killed by a gunman at a Black Lives Matter rally. Obama condemned the officers' slayings as "an act not just of demented violence but of racial hatred."[524] At a memorial service for the dead officers, he said, "I'm here to insist that we are not as divided as we seem."

Despite the president's words, and despite the fact that the majority of violent crimes by Blacks are against Blacks and by whites are against whites, the notion that race relations had deteriorated on his watch was firmly in place by the end of Obama's time in the White House.

---

523 https://www.latimes.com/nation/la-na-obama-race-reax-20170816-story.html
524 https://obamawhitehouse.archives.gov/the-press-office/2016/07/12/remarks-president-memorial-service-fallen-dallas-police-officers

Income Inequality

Income Inequality

President Obama was widely credited with bringing about income gains for Americans during the economic recovery of 2009–2015. But an analysis by economist Emmanuel Saez showed that income recipients did not share equally in the pie.[525]

During the six-year period, according to Saez's estimates, the top 1 percent of earners benefited from a disproportionate share of market income gains. While Americans in the bottom nine-tenths of income distribution saw average market income gains of 4 percent, the top 1 percent had gains of 24 percent. "Market Income" means non-governmental sources of income, which excludes such means as public assistance, Social Security, and food stamps.

Income Stagnation

In 2016, the real median household income of Americans was recorded as $61,383, down from $61,932 in 2008.[526] That was a drop of about 1 percent, virtually stagnant over Obama's eight years in office.

Gini

The Gini Index is a tool used by economists and others as a measurement of income inequality in a given country and over time. The Gini ranges from zero to one, and the higher the number, the more unequal the distribution of income.

At the outset of Obama's presidency in 2009, the Gini was .468. It was .481 at the end of the Obama years, in 2016.[527]

---

525   https://www.brookings.edu/opinions/income-growth-has-been-negligible-but-surprise-inequality-has-narrowed-since-2007/

526   https://www.deptofnumbers.com/income/us/

527   https://www.census.gov/data/tables/time-series/demo/income-poverty/historical-income-inequality.html

Among industrialized OECD nations in 2015, the United States was, in terms of income inequality, in the bottom 20 percent.[528] Only Turkey, Chile, Costa Rica, and South Africa had higher Gini indices.

528   https://data.oecd.org/inequality/income-inequality.htm

WEALTH INEQUALITY

Top 1 Percent Ownership

The Federal Reserve's triennial Survey of Consumer Finances found that in 2007, the richest 1 percent of the American population owned 33.6 percent of the country's total wealth.[529] In 2016, the top 1 percent owned 38.5 percent of the nation's wealth. The average wealth of the bottom 99 percent dropped by $4,500 between 2007 and 2016, while the average wealth of the top 1 percent rose by $4.9 million over the same period.[530]

Median household net worth, 2007 to 2016 (in 2016 dollars):[531]

2007: $139,700

2010: $85,400

2013: $83,700

2016: $97,300

Median Wealth

In mid-2017, the year Obama's second term ended, the United States ranked 21st in median wealth per adult, among 171 countries, according to the Global Wealth Report by the Credit Suisse Research Institute.[532] The U.S. fell behind Taiwan and Singapore, and, as one might expect, Switzerland, Norway, Australia, and Japan. Alongside the U.S. were Austria and Greece.

529 https://www.federalreserve.gov/econres/scf-previous-surveys.htm

530 https://jacobinmag.com/2017/12/obama-foreclosure-crisis-wealth-inequality

531 https://www.newstrategist.com/median-net-worth-97300-in-2016/

532 https://www.credit-suisse.com/media/assets/corporate/docs/about-us/research/publications/global-wealth-report-2017-en.pdf

Infrastructure

Every four years, the American Society of Civil Engineers (ASCE) grades various categories of the nation's infrastructure, and then assigns a grade point average (GPA). The categories are: Aviation, Bridges, Dams, Drinking Water, Energy, Hazardous Waste, Inland Waterways, Levees, Ports, Public Parks, Rail, Roads, Schools, Transit, Solid Waste, and Wastewater.

In 2009 the GPA was D; in 2013, D+; and in 2017, D+.[533] Some categories improved while others further deteriorated, but the overall score throughout the entire Obama administration was either D or D+.

533 https://www.infrastructurereportcard.org/making-the-grade/report-card-history/

Mortgage Fee Reduction

Little more than a week before President Trump was inaugurated, the Obama administration's Department of Housing and Urban Development announced it would reduce annual fees on most first-time mortgages insured by the Federal Housing Administration.[534] This action would save the typical first-time FHA-insured mortgagee approximately $500 a year the first year of the mortgage. The move was reversed by Trump as one of his first acts following the inauguration—on the same day as the inauguration, in fact.

U.S. Senate Minority Leader Chuck Schumer condemned the reversal of the Obama administration's enlightened policy decision. "It took only an hour after [Trump's] positive words on the inaugural platform for his actions to ring hollow," Schumer said.[535] "One hour after talking about helping working people and ending the cabal in Washington that hurts people, he signs a regulation that makes it more expensive for new homeowners to buy mortgages."

534 https://www.reuters.com/article/us-usa-housing-premiums/as-trump-takes-over-u-s-ends-plan-to-cut-mortgage-premiums-idUSKBN1542IQ
535 https://edition.cnn.com/2017/01/23/politics/donald-trump-first-action-hud/index.html

Minimum Wage

Despite issuing pleas to the Republican-controlled Congress to increase the federal minimum wage, Obama left the White House as only the third president since 1938—the year the wage was enacted— to fail to achieve a hike.[536] The minimum wage remained at $7.25 the entire two terms of the Obama presidency.

536 https://obamawhitehouse.archives.gov/sites/default/files/minimum_wage/6_ october_2016_min_wage_report-final.pdf; https://thehill.com/policy/finance/230168- obama-asks-congress-to-hike-minimum-wage; https://www.theguardian.com/ business/2016/sep/05/barack-obama-us-minimum-wage-republicans-tom-perez

Quality of Life

The United States dropped nine places in the United Nations' Human Development Index (HDI) between 2009 and 2017. The U.S. was ranked 4th among all member nations in 2009, and fell to 13th place in 2017.[537] According to the UN,

"The HDI was created to emphasize that people and their capabilities should be the ultimate criteria for assessing the development of a country, not economic growth alone. [...] The Human Development Index (HDI) is a summary measure of average achievement in key dimensions of human development: a long and healthy life, being knowledgeable and have a decent standard of living. [...] The health dimension is assessed by life expectancy at birth, the education dimension is measured by mean of years of schooling for adults aged 25 years and more and expected years of schooling for children of school entering age. The standard of living dimension is measured by gross national income per capita. [...] The scores for the three HDI dimension indices are then aggregated into a composite index using geometric mean." [538]

537 http://hdr.undp.org/sites/default/files/reports/270/hdr_2010_en_complete_reprint. pdf; http://hdr.undp.org/sites/default/files/2018_human_development_statistical_ update.pdf

538 http://hdr.undp.org/en/content/human-development-index-hdi

ABOUT THE AUTHOR

Robert Eisenberg, born and raised in Omaha, received a BA in political science from Columbia University and an MA in government from Harvard. He earned a law degree from Creighton University, where he later served as a professor. He has also lectured at Harvard and the University of Nebraska. Eisenberg is the author of *Boychiks in the Hood*, an exploration of contemporary Hasidic culture, described by the *New York Times Sunday Book Review* as "a rich collection of anecdotes, religious history and thumbnail portraits." He currently resides in New York City.